# school communities

DREW

Safer School Communities: Working In Partnership
With School-Based Police Officers

Middlesex: Middlesex                    190475001X

# *Safer* school communities

working in partnership with school-based police officers

## Andrew Briers

MIDDLESEX
UNIVERSITY
PRESS

First published in 2004 by Middlesex University Press

Copyright © Dr Andrew Briers 2004

ISBN  1 904750 01 X

A CIP catalogue record for this book is available from
The British Library


Design by Helen Taylor

Printed and bound in the UK by Hobbs the Printers, Hampshire.



Middlesex University Press would like to express thanks to Northumbria Police
Authority and the London Borough of Enfield Education Service for the images
they supplied for the front cover.

Middlesex University Press, Queensway, Enfield, Middlesex EN4 3SF

Tel: +44 (0)20 8411 5734 : +44 (0)20 8880 4262  Fax: +44 (0)20 8411 5736

www.mupress.co.uk

# Contents

# Foreword

THIS BOOK WAS INITIALLY INTENDED TO ACT as a guide for the school officers who now work full time in secondary schools across the country under the banner of the Safer School Partnership (SSP), a government initiative supported by the Youth Justice Board. However, what has emerged as a consequence of researching this area of work is that there is a far wider need for teachers, pupils, police support personnel, parents and members of the community to have an understanding of the work which is involved in developing a Safer School Partnership and how this can best be achieved and built upon.

There are roles emerging from this book, not only for the police officers working in the school community but also for a variety of other agencies and supporters of the partnership who, in unison, can create a safer school environment for the whole community. To achieve this there are a number of fundamental steps which need to take place to ensure that these processes will materialise. This book explains the history of schools liaison work in the UK and how the role of police in schools has changed from a purely educational role to a much more complex one of enforcement and advice – as well as offering educational inputs and being the traditional role model.

This process of change is not an easy one, although several pilot sites around the country have helped to highlight initial good practice as well as areas of concern in implementing the Safer School Partnership. Research from abroad, in particular America, reveals that similar problems were experienced in their school programmes when they were first established in the late eighties.

What this book does is to build upon such work from around the country and abroad and provide a guide for all interested parties to develop a Safer School Partnership; secondly, it may inspire individuals to explore ways in which they can contribute to such a programme. In the past twelve months, police officers and their partners have come up with a number of excellent initiatives, which they have developed to help create a safer school and meet the aims and objectives of the Safer School Partnership.

i

It is hoped that this book will inspire more people to look for innovative ways to improve the partnership and to involve more partners in its daily programme. The Safer School Partnership is an excellent tool, not only for addressing youth crime, but also in understanding youth culture and involving our youth in issues that directly affect them.

To assist partners further, a training manual has been designed to allow all participants to undertake training that will assist them with the development of the partnership with modules including problem solving, risk assessments, dealing with disruptive pupils, safer routes to schools, drug awareness and supporting young victims of crime.

Never before have police officers had such a demanding and complex role within the community; it is with this in mind that all within the partnership can draw upon the experiences and lessons from this book to bring about safer school communities across the nation.

# Acknowledgements

I WOULD LIKE TO THANK THE Fulbright Commission for giving me the opportunity to travel to the USA on a Police Fulbright Fellowship Award and the Metropolitan Police Service for giving their full support to my research. I also owe a debt of gratitude to Professor Peter Newby who supervised my PhD at Middlesex University. Thanks are also due to the team at Middlesex University Press for working with me to bring this book to publication. Last but not least I would like to thank my wife Michelle for supporting me throughout my period of study and research.

# CHAPTER 1

# Youth Crime

## Introduction

Now, more than ever, youth violence appears on the news and across the tabloids as an escalating problem, which needs to be addressed. It would appear from the intense media coverage that youth crime is an epidemic sweeping across the nation. Every day there are reports of robberies and burglaries being carried out across the country, centred mainly on inner-city areas by gangs of juveniles. Many of the victims explain that they have been assaulted, robbed or abused by children as young as ten – and often during the school day, when the pupils should be engaged at school.

The Metropolitan Police have concluded, from analysing their own data taken from a current initiative 'Operation Safer Streets', that between half and three-quarters of street crimes are committed by juveniles; and that of those arrested for street crime, nearly three-quarters were not previously known to the criminal justice agencies. It seems to be a worrying trend that more young people are coming to notice on the first occasion for street crime as opposed to less serious offences.

It is a fact that, in London, street crimes such as robbery tend to be concentrated in the more deprived areas of the city; it is also a fact that it is the visible minorities that are concentrated in these same deprived inner city areas, and that they are the fastest growing section of the population.

The Youth Justice Board (YJB) have taken the lead in this apparent war on juvenile offending and have done much to highlight the true extent and impact of youth offending in light of the youth justice reforms that were set out in the Crime and Disorder Act 1998. One of the YJB's main concerns is that, due to over-zealous reporting by the media industry, the public perception of youth crime is far greater than that which actually exists. In particular, the YJB highlights the availability of relevant statistics, which include the British Crime Survey, police-reported crime figures, Home Office statistics on cautions and convictions as well as a MORI survey of youth crime on behalf of the Youth Justice Board. Although the information that these surveys provide differs, they do all show that youth crime is either declining or constant and not out of control – as is the public's perception.

There has been a noticeable rise in the number of violent crimes such as robbery and antisocial behaviour, and it may be that crimes such as these are making the headlines due to their shocking nature. The MORI survey reinforces this belief, revealing that self-reported offending levels by school-age children have remained fairly constant since 1999. In its defence, the survey is open to abuse from pupils who can either fail to report an offence – or, conversely, report one in an attempt to exaggerate or boast about their activities.

However, what is of concern to many teachers, school support workers and police liaison officers is that there are a significant number of crimes that are committed by children on the way to school, at school and again on the way home from school, as well as after school hours which either never get dealt with by the relevant authority or reported to the police. First-hand accounts, and numerous reports from colleagues in the professional arena of working with children, confirm this suspicion; our collective inability as a society at large to tackle this is resulting in a culture where children are too scared to travel on buses to school in case they are robbed for their mobile phone or pocket money. Such children inevitably become the repeat victims of these crimes and are, unsurprisingly, afraid of reporting these incidents for fear of retaliation from the perpetrators. These incidents are real and occur on a regular basis; the suspects and victims are all too aware of the 'rules', which apply both to the street and to the school.

The following example is taken from a group discussion about crime and consequences at a Junior Mixed Attendance Centre by a group of fifteen attendees during a lesson as part of their court order.

Martin: *Listen, Yeah, when you walk down the street right you got to know what you are doing.*

Instructor: What do you mean?

Martin: *Well if some guy is thinking about "jacking" you yeah, then you need to know what to do. You got to look after yourself. If you get jacked it's your own fault you deserve it.*

Instructor: Have you ever been "jacked"?

Martin: *Yeah a group of kids jumped me and "teeved" my phone. I just went round the corner and "jacked" another kid; it's just how it is.*

Instructor: Why is it your own fault if you get "jacked"?

General laughter from the class.

Martin: *Cos it just is, that's how things happen on the street, you got to wise up and if you belong to the street like us then that's how it is. If you are too flash, or got clothes and gear or a neat phone then you better hang on to it.*

What happens in the school is often played out in the community after school hours; and conversely what happens within the community at night and at weekends is invariably taken into the confines of the school. Teachers are often left to deal with incidents of fighting, robberies and antisocial behaviour which have been left unresolved from the night before. There is a need to redress the balance and define clear guidelines for behaviour, which apply to all children whether at school, or in the wider community.

## Youth issues

There have been a number of reports on current initiatives that are relevant to reducing criminality, many of which have been adopted as features of good working practice. (See, for example, Graham and Bowling, 1996).

In particular the National Association for the Care and Resettlement of Offenders (NACRO) committee on Children Schools and Crime (1998), published a report outlining four key links between schooling and crime:

● Antisocial and criminal behaviour in schools, (Routledge, 1994)

- The area of attachment and achievement in school as highlighted by Farrington (1996)
- The area of absenteeism and the belief that links exist between truancy and the onset of offending. (Graham and Bowling, 1996)
- The issue of exclusion and its relation with pupils offending as highlighted by the Audit Commission's report, Misspent Youth (1996)

Studies carried out by MORI for the Youth Justice Board, (2001), found that one in four school pupils across the country states that they have committed a crime and that one in five has armed him/herself. A staggering 23% of excluded pupils state that they have been in possession of a gun and 44% state that they have carried a knife.

There are many agencies that are working, both alone and in partnership, to try and stem the numbers of young people who are finding themselves caught up in the criminal justice process and inevitably incarcerated in one of the country's Young Offender Institutions. Some schemes have proved more successful than others at tackling youth crime from both a proactive and reactive role, and many of these are highlighted in the following pages.

The Youth Justice Board is the central driving force behind tackling youth crime in the country and recently commissioned 'Communities that Care' to look at the risk and protective factors that lead to youth crime and to identify any effective interventions to prevent it. The report highlights risk and protective factors for youth crime into four main areas: the family, school, community and those which are individual, personal and related to peer-group experiences.

## Risk factors

Family risk factors include: poor parental supervision and discipline, family conflict, a family history of criminal activity, parental attitudes that condone antisocial behaviour, low income poor housing and a large family size.

Risk factors in the school context include low achievement beginning in primary school, aggressive behaviour (including bullying), lack of commitment to school, (including truancy) and school disorganisation, all of which increase the likelihood that young people exposed to them will become involved in crime.

Within the community, the risk factors identified by research are: living in a disadvantaged neighbourhood, community disorganisation and neglect, availability of drugs and high turnover and lack of neighbourhood attachment.

Risk factors for youth crime that are essentially individual include: hyperactivity and impulsivity, low intelligence and cognitive impairment, alienation and lack of social commitment, attitudes that condone offending and drug misuse and early involvement in crime and drug misuse. Friendships with peers involved in crime and drug misuse also increase.

*Youth Justice Board November 2001*

## Protection factors

Factors that will protect against involvement in youth crime, even in the presence of the risk factors listed above, include: female gender, a resilient temperament, a sense of self-efficacy, a positive, outgoing disposition and high intelligence. Social bonding and the promotion within the family, school and community of healthy standards will also act as protective factors.

*Youth Justice Board, November 2001*

It therefore becomes apparent that, to help protect children from these risks, there is a collective responsibility of parents, teachers and the community in general to lead by example and to set out clear guidelines of how children should behave. School is naturally one arena, which can significantly influence the lives of children and help shape and develop them, and act as a means of protection against the associated risk factors.

Schools have the potential as a focus for crime prevention. They provide regular access to students throughout the developmental years, and perhaps the only consistent access to large numbers of the most crime-prone young children in the early school years; they are staffed with individuals paid to help youth develop as healthy, happy, productive citizens; and the community usually supports schools' efforts to socialise youth. Many of the precursors of delinquent behaviour are school-related and therefore likely to be amenable to change through school-based intervention.

*Denise C Gottfredson, 1998*

There are currently a number of initiatives being adopted by the government to combat children behaving badly at school; funding has been made available to target key areas such as truancy, exclusions and bad behaviour. The strategy is to support teachers, by spotting problems early and intervening before truancy and exclusion is established in a school. This will be achieved in a variety of ways, including advice from specialists and additional training for teachers as part of their professional development.

Additional support will be available from Behaviour and Education Support Teams (BEST), who bring together specialists such as social workers, health officials to support the needs of the pupils, parents and teachers. After-school activities will enable pupils to engage in additional learning for themselves and their families and forge closer links between the school and community and be a focal point where parents can learn more about the behaviour of their child in school and be a positive influence. Summer activities are offered to children, to keep them engaged and active over the holidays; many of the wide-ranging activities are targeted at pupils who are excluded or who truant and those identified as being at risk of offending. Other pupils can benefit from key workers who work with them in school helping them to cope with the constant pressures of school life and the demands of homework and punctuality.

A summary of other measures that are currently used to reduce youth crime includes: parenting orders, youth inclusion programmes, education training and employment programmes and intensive supervision and surveillance programmes.

One additional area of support proposed for teachers is the introduction of police officers in schools, who will be permanently attached to a specific secondary school with a cluster of primary schools. This is a new initiative, which has been introduced into a number of schools in the UK. It differs markedly from other forms of intervention, in that it intends to tackle the issue of crime and bad behaviour in schools in a proactive way, whilst offering support for the teachers and victims. It is the emergence of two cultures: the police, on one hand, and the teaching profession on the other; their cultures, beliefs and values are markedly different.

## History of police involvement in schools

The first police juvenile liaison scheme was introduced in Liverpool in

1949 as a way of dealing with 'incipient delinquency'. In 1954, the Advisory Council on the Treatment of Offenders considered the impact of these schemes, as did the chief officers of police at an annual conference.

Not everybody was convinced of the work of police juvenile liaisons and the Committee on Children and Young Persons (Ingleby Committee, 1960), made it clear that they did not recommend their general adoption despite some of the good work they had produced. Consequently the number of schemes ceased to grow until the 1968 Home Office White Paper *Children in Trouble*, which gave recognition to the work of the police juvenile liaison schemes. Nearly twenty years later, the scheme had expanded to seventeen areas in England and Wales.

The role of the officer was to establish 'good relationships with schools, shops, firms, youth organisations and social agencies'. Through these contacts the officer would make it his or her duty to get to know all the young people and to be kept informed of their behaviour, especially where it bordered on the delinquent. Those children who showed signs of delinquency ('petty thieves, those mixing in delinquent or undesirable company, and young hooligans', as Taylor refers to them) could be referred to him for supervision.

> 'This may involve the officer alerting the authorities that are in contact with the child to the need for special attention, introducing children into youth clubs and similar organisations, and visiting the home in order to encourage the parents to assist in forestalling a delinquent career.'
>
> Taylor, M 1971

In 1984, The Advisory Committee on Police in Schools (ACPS) looked at some of the issues being raised by the increasing involvement of police in schools. It attempted to look at what police teachers actually did in the schools and whether their existence in the classroom was actually justified.

It then proposed guidelines for the way in which schools should interact with police when dealing with issues around investigation of offences and crime reporting as well as information exchange. In addition the report attempted to understand the effect of such 'multi-agency policing' upon schools and education.

More recent guidance for officers working within schools focuses upon officers who visit schools on an ad hoc basis. Current Metropolitan

Police publications include *Guidelines for police officers on working with education establishments and community groups* (1998) and *Police response to incidents in schools* (2001).

The Kent, Thames Valley, Nottinghamshire and Northumbria constabularies have developed their own policies and practices in this area, but they all share a common theme of early intervention with young people in an attempt to divert them from crime.

A number of good examples where partnerships such as these are working well are highlighted in the DfEE document entitled *Together we can tackle it: a checklist for police and schools working together to tackle truancy, crime and disorder.* (2001).

These include:

- Head teachers in Kent working with partners in the local community to help pupils who had been identified as truants and being at risk from exclusion
- Thames Valley educational social workers, police and schools have a partnership approach to dealing with truants by organising home visits
- London police have set up Acceptable Behaviour Contracts with troublesome youngsters in partnership with local housing offices
- Throughout London police, educational welfare officers and youth workers perform joint truancy sweeps on a regular basis with great success

Many other projects are outlined in a Home Office research study (No 161, 1996). This looks at work which attempts to prevent young people from becoming involved in crime. It focuses on five key areas identified by Graham and Bowling.

- Strengthening families – parent training, family centres
- Strengthening schools – strategies to prevent truanting
- Protecting young people from the influence of delinquents in their peer group from high-risk activities
- Harnessing the sources of social control within the criminal justice system to the more informal sources of control found among families, schools and neighbours
- Preparing young people for fully independent and responsible adulthood

What, however, is missing from all of the police-based approaches is a co-ordinated and effective evaluation of their processes and outcomes, which would enable police forces to see for themselves how effective such schemes can be.

The Youth Justice Board for England and Wales is currently working, in conjunction with the Association of Chief Police Officers (ACPO), to develop a more coherent strategy for preventing youth crime through closer working of police, schools and Youth Offending Teams (YOTs). This strategy will be submitted to the Home Secretary under section 41 of the Crime and Disorder Act 1998. Traditionally, police interaction with schools has been focused on crime reduction and preventing children from offending by presenting classroom-based talks on such issues as crime and consequences, personal safety, drugs education and bullying. It is fair to say that many of the officers engaged in this type of schoolwork were in the twilight of their career and often regarded by operational officers as 'not performing real police work'. As the divide between the work of the school officers and other departments in the police service grew – and many school officers became isolated in their work – many police authorities stopped supporting their role and subsequently disbanded school officer provision.

This process was further compounded by work conducted at Roehampton Institute, University of Surrey. Research into the role of police education in schools on behalf of the ACPO Drugs subcommittee concluded that much of the work of the schools involvement officers around drugs education was questionable (O'Connor, 2001).

Much of the research centred on the officer's ability to deliver classroom presentations and the content of the lessons. These officers are not trained teachers and the instruction they receive prior to entering schools is limited and very basic, so it is not surprising that the analysis was critical of their work. The role of the schools involvement officer needs to be radically reassessed from being purely an educational role to becoming a more proactive one; they should be able to engage not only with the pupils, but also the staff, parents, community and school as a whole. This will enable officers to build up stronger links with young people and help to understand some of the issues which they are facing in today's society, especially those which cause the most conflict with police and inevitably lead to the alienation of the youth culture.

## Stop and search

Top of the agenda for many young people is the issue of 'stop and search'. In my role as officer in charge of an Attendance Centre for the Home Office, I educate and rehabilitate young offenders, through a series of workshops based around their offending, in order to successfully reintegrate them back into society. One of the many topics we discuss is based on the police use of stop and search amongst young people. This is the most controversial of all the lessons which they take part in; in no other lesson are they so expressive in their thoughts and feelings on the way in which police conduct themselves around young people.

There have been numerous studies, which capture the feelings of young people towards police. One in particular, the Home Office research study *Tell Them So They Listen: Messages from Young People in Custody* (2000), contains interviews with young people already in the criminal justice system. They highlighted their concerns that people in authority need to tackle racism more effectively and ensure fair, respectful and appropriate treatment for young black people; and that particular attention needed to be paid towards improving relations between the police and young people.

A further study by the Home Office (*Police Stops and Searches: Lessons from a Programme of Research*, 2001) reveals the views of people who are stopped and searched. These include the feeling of being victimised by the police because of their ethnic background and the general attitude of the police towards them, especially by young officers who are often seen as patronising, arrogant, aggressive and intimidating. Further feelings describe a general mistrust of the police and a belief that the police will fabricate evidence and display racist behaviour to goad people and inflame situations, which inevitably results in conflict. Because of these experiences, which many young people state are played out in numerous inner city areas, they refuse to co-operate with the police and instead view them as the enemy. Consequently, crimes that occur between young people are rarely reported to police; the young people will often prefer to deal with the problem themselves. This can lead to escalating forms of violence, which can be seen in many of the nation's school playgrounds.

I have already alluded to the growing concern at the extent of youth crime in the country and these feelings are reflected in the Metropolitan Police Statement of Aims, which states that dealing with youth crime is, alongside countering terrorism, its number one priority. What is now needed is a policy that will clearly demonstrate how police can tackle this growing tide of youth crime. Initial suggestions highlight the need for closer supervision of children; suitable activities which will engage them both in and out of school; work around raising the attainment of pupils and remedies to the rising number of exclusions and truants who inevitably become victims of crime – or who themselves are lured into a life of crime.

One solution is that a new breed of school officers can, in partnership with other agencies such as schools and Youth Offender Teams (YOTs), tackle many of these issues successfully through a clearly defined programme of intervention. My own experiences as a teacher and police officer led me to develop such a programme which I could deliver in schools, in partnership with other agencies, to improve the links between schools and police and to provide the basis for some meaningful work; this will ultimately lead to a reduction in general crime and disorder in and around schools.

Chapter 2 considers the work that I undertook as a schools officer based full time in a school in the Metropolitan Police District. It considers some of the main advantages and disadvantages of the pilot scheme and offers some useful feedback from teachers and pupils about their perceptions of the scheme.

# School-based policing

## Pilot scheme

The initial pilot scheme in London was set up as part of a final submission for a Single Regeneration Bid, on behalf of the local borough (police division) partnership. The purpose of this bid was to regenerate the area through community involvement and empowerment and to fulfil its vision to transform the area into a 'thriving community where people want to live, work, study and succeed.' (London Council Report, 2000).

## The aims of the initiative were to:

> Develop trust and enhance relationships between school, police and the community
>
> Represent the Metropolitan Police Service (MPS) in the community
>
> Develop and implement partnership activities with the local school, to reduce crime and disorder in the area.

A list of strategies which were employed by the police, in order to fulfil the aims of the project, is shown in Figure 1.

## Evaluation

The scheme was evaluated by the Department for Education and Skills (DfES), but not published; however, qualitative evidence gained from questionnaires and interviews from staff, pupils and parents at the school, combined with the officer's own experiences, reveal the project as being potentially very successful.

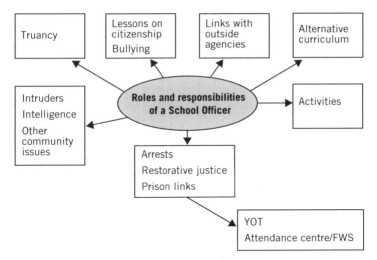

**Figure 1  Responsibilities of a School Officer**

The main areas highlighted as being successful can be measured alongside the current government's policies which include the following:

- School community links: raising pupil's motivation, expectation and achievement
- Reducing truancy
- Reducing bullying
- Personal, Social and Health Education (PSHE)
- Citizenship
- Public reassurance
- Fear of crime
- Reducing youth crime.

## Areas of success

### Cadet unit

The formation of a police cadet unit within the school; this had over forty members from years 7 and 8, whose ethnic mix reflected that of the school, where over 57 different languages are spoken. The implications with regard to ethnic recruitment within the police service speak for themselves and this unit serves as a feeding ground for the popular expanding borough-wide cadet units, which number approximately twenty-two out of the thirty-two London boroughs. This is an initiative which was highlighted by the shadow Home Secretary as being a key role in 'boosting police recruitment from the ethnic minorities'. (Bamber, 2000).

## Truancy

The number of truants who were returned to the school on a daily basis was a good indicator of the extent of truancy that exists within schools; combined with regular truancy sweeps under the Crime and Disorder Act this provided a larger-scale picture of truancy across the borough. A number of teachers commented on the reduction in truancy in their questionnaire responses. 'Punctuality has improved', 'A reduction in truancy and truants are picked up more easily' (Briers, 2003).

## Arrests

There were over 40 arrests made over a period of two school terms, which were effected either directly by the officer or as a result of information from the officer. The vast majority of these offences were for robberies, which were often carried out against other pupils in the school.

## Intelligence

Numerous forms of intelligence were gathered from pupils, parents, teachers and members of the local community; this enabled the police to keep informed as to what was happening in the local community and culminated in the identification of a number of robbery suspects from video cameras.

## Links with outside agencies

The officer was able to forge links with various outside agencies which included the drugs counsellor, and visits to the school by a serving inmate from a nearby adult prison under the guidance of supervised staff in an effort to educate the pupils about the consequences of their actions. (Lloyd, 1996)

## Links with the community

Good links were forged with a premiership football club who attended the school and provided football coaching for the pupils through their community programme. The officer was able to use a local church youth group to deliver Christian-based workshops on bullying to Year 7 pupils; the officer followed this up with several talks to youth groups at local churches at their Sunday morning services. After-school activities included a swimming programme, which taught over 180 children in the local borough to swim after several tragic deaths by drowning in a nearby river. All sponsorship was raised through the police with local partnerships in order to fund the venture.

## Feedback from staff and pupils

This was in general extremely positive and the presence of an officer on the school site was generally very welcome. However, not everybody understood the role of the officer and there appeared to be some confusion about exactly what the officer could and could not do. Most teachers saw the role as being a 'visible deterrent to discourage and deal with intruders, drug dealing, bullying, vandalism, potential troublemakers, petty crime, misbehaviour and theft.' (Briers, 2003). Several teachers stated that they would like to see the officer more involved in curricular work in the classroom and on school trips, where they could socialise with the pupils away from a school setting.

The vast majority felt much safer with a police officer on site 'I do feel safer having the police around despite having mixed feelings about the police.' (Briers, 2003). Several stated that this presence acted as a deterrent to outsiders. With a few notable exceptions, over 70% of the staff surveyed stated that the police officer had helped them in a variety of ways which included 'calming aggressive students, dealing with intruders, offering advice, helping out with both school and outside activities, acting in a consultative role, dealing with thefts of mobile phones and giving talks.'

## Partnership problems

Conversely, only three members of staff made negative comments, which all centred on the arrest of a pupil where they felt the officer acted inappropriately; this, consequently, gave rise to some problems within the partnership. Other positive comments from teachers, however, included the following:

> (The officer should be) allowed to be more active within the work of the school yet still maintaining powers of police and arrest.
>
> I feel that you should have a more 'seen' role, where you are more 'in-charge' and are able to act as any police officer on duty and not always have to negotiate arrests with the head in such detail.

> (The officer should have) power to take into custody any
> perpetrators of offences – drug pushing, bullying,
> threatening behaviour, stealing and fighting. The police
> should be dealing with criminal activities in accordance
> with the law and not what the school deems.
>
> *Briers, 2003*

## Police culture

Another barrier experienced by the officer was the issue of police culture and the extent to which other officers consider this role as being both serious and worthwhile. This feeling was partly due to their lack of understanding, but also a lack of awareness of the pilot project's existence. On several occasions police would arrive at the school unaware that there was an officer based at the school. Once the role was more widely known, and local officers became aware of the advantages that this could afford them, then several good arrests were made and valuable information was obtained and shared. (Briers, 2003)

Similar schemes were replicated in other areas of the country; although independent of each other, they sought to reduce youth crime through a variety of aims by placing police officers in school on a full-time basis.

## Thames Valley Police

In September 1997, a community support team was formed to work on the Bretch Hill Estate in Banbury. Its aim was to develop a 'locally based, multi-agency, problem-solving team to tackle a failing community'. The work of the team received national and international recognition for its achievements in reducing crime and the fear of crime, along with notable successes in working in partnership with schools where it was recognised that significant reductions were being made in youth crime.

The success of the pilot scheme lay behind the idea of dispensing with the traditional approach to school liaison work outlined earlier in this book and focusing on the placement of School Beat Officers to police the local school communities. The officers in partnership with the school concentrated their efforts on tackling the six strongest risk factors in the lives of those young people, which inevitably led to criminality. These six factors were:

- Truancy
- Exclusion
- Poor parental supervision
- Conflict in the home
- Friends and siblings in trouble
- Poor school performance.

Chipping Norton School was an example of just such a scheme in North Oxfordshire, where an officer has been stationed on site, sharing an office with the school's heads of year. Although not an area that is known as a trouble hotspot (in fact, it is officially one of the safest places to live in England!) the officer still has a full schedule whilst engaged at the school.

He is called in to help with serious discipline problems; if a crime is committed on site, he is there to deal with it; if a crime is committed off site, and one of the pupils is suspected, he is the best person to deal with it, because the chances are he already knows the young person involved. He helps tackle truancy; he gives talks on drugs and alcohol, on safe driving and the criminal justice system. Oh, and later this summer he is helping on a school outdoor pursuits trip with staff and pupils. (Weale S, 2002)

## Metropolitan Police, Southwark

Initially the Home Office was reserved on the idea of placing police officers full time in schools, despite suggestions from the chief constable of Thames Valley Police that this was the best mode of deployment.

The government's response at the time was expressed by Mike O'Brien, Parliamentary Under-Secretary of State, who stated 'Part of the process of ensuring the police enter into a close relationship with young people is having officers present in schools. But I don't think most people would want to see a police officer stationed all day in a school.' (Mulraney S, 2000)

The London Borough of Southwark was another pioneer of the scheme and hit the headlines after a policewoman was brought into one of its schools less than a mile from the spot where the young victim Damilola Taylor was stabbed to death. The school in which she worked had been the subject of rising crime, with reports of robbery, bullying, harassment and thefts. The head teacher was very positive towards the scheme and hoped that by having a school officer 'people will be deterred from thinking that they can come down to the school and attack our kids.' (Hurst J, 2001)

Initial signs highlighted the scheme as successful: crime which could be associated with the school declined by 95%; emergency calls to the school dropped from more than forty in the four months prior to the scheme to zero after the initiation of the scheme.

The scheme quickly spread to other schools in the borough; although in its early stages, there were a number of positive as well as negative aspects to be gleaned from the process. Some of these were expressed initially by head teachers within the borough, two of which were published in *The Teacher* magazine, September 2002. Below are extracts from the article.

### Police watch

**Is the principle of having a police presence in schools a good idea?**

Two teachers debate a contentious issue.

*'Our founding principles at the Charter School were to be fully inclusive and to serve the needs of our immediate local community. As part of this initial pledge, we were pleased to welcome our local police liaison officers to planning meetings from the outset and have worked in close partnership to expand the range and depth of our association.'*

Charter School, London Borough of Southwark

*'I, like every other teacher, parent or ex-pupil, understand the importance of establishing a safe and secure learning environment in school. However, while schools should have access to the essential police services when they are needed, these services should not be a permanent fixture in the school environment. If and when we need the police, we know where to find them'*

Kingsdale School, Dulwich

The Teacher *magazine, September 2002*

## Police in schools: for and against

There is some concern from educationalists in Britain that the presence of police in schools could bring about the kind of situation that presently exists in a number of schools in the US where, according to Steve Doughty of the *Daily Mail* (2001), 'schools operate like armed camps or prisons with armed guards and metal detectors at every door'. The Metropolitan Police confirmed that they intend to build upon the initial pilot project and extend the scheme to an entire inner city area. This news has been met with a mixed reception amongst the teaching staff although Nigel de Gruchy, when leader of the NASUWT, welcomed the plan. 'It's a good idea and it is about 20 years too late,' he said. 'We could do with more police officers in schools: there is an enormous amount of crime that is not dealt with in schools that the police do have the power to deal with outside'. (*Daily Mail*, 2001)

Not every educationalist shares these sentiments. Nick Seaton, a spokesman for the Campaign for Real Education, describes the prospect of police in schools as 'tragic'.

The Conservative party have seized the opportunity to criticise the government for letting teenage criminal behaviour spiral out of control. Ann Widdecombe, when Shadow Home Secretary, has stated, 'Saying that we need policemen in schools is not the answer to the problem. It is putting a sticking plaster on it. We need to deal with the disease'. This statement, however, appears to contradict her own initiative to have a police cadet unit in every secondary school. (*Sunday Telegraph*, 25 June 2000).

What is encouraging is that the scheme has the support of the teaching unions who are aware of the escalating number of violent acts in schools and understand the potential benefits of placing police in schools to work with children.

In a BBC News programme, *Talking Point*, broadcast on 16 May 2001, listeners were given the opportunity to debate the subject 'Police in schools: is it a good idea?'. The responses came from across the world and a selection of the comments, which reflect the differences of opinions that exist are outlined below. A more comprehensive selection can be obtained from the BBC News *Talking Point* website at http://news.bbc.co.uk/1/hi/talking_point

The next step will be policemen in every home to make sure we behave ourselves in a fashion that they deem 'acceptable'. State influence in our lives is already too great-we should be reducing it, not increasing.

*Mark B, England*

It is a shame that it has come to this, but there is a need. If I were a parent, I would not complain-the police are hardly going to cause trouble. A heavy-handed approach is needed to protect our children; they are our most precious asset. A 10 year old was killed-surely that is as sign that police presence-however drastic it may seem-is required-so no-one else has to pay for crime with their life. Better police than the situation they have in some USA schools-where all pupils must have see through bags to prevent them bringing weapons into school. It's just a shame police can't make all the children work in the school as well.

*John Hutchence, UK*

The problem is that most school age criminals know they are so over-protected by the law that they are virtually untouchable. Unfortunately this is the flipside of the well-meaning efforts of child protection lobbies, the guilty derive immunity from the protection of the innocent.

*Bobby, UK*

Crazy! Big Brother is here to stay. What a pitiful control freaked, bunch of sheep we are. Who needs a general election? Ask the cops!

*John, UK*

If successive governments over the years had not eroded the powers of teachers in respect of punishing kids, there would not be the need for police officers to be stationed in schools. But it's a damn good idea!!

*Rob Elliot, Kosovo*

*BBC News programme, Talking Point*

# CHAPTER 3

# School Resource Officers in the USA

## History of school liaisons in the USA

This chapter considers the role of schools officers in the United States of America and how they have established and developed their roles and responsibilities over a number of years. There are a number of valuable lessons that programmes in the UK can learn from the processes that many US police/school partnerships built upon in the early stages of their development. In 2002, as part of my PhD comparative research project, I travelled to Colorado, USA, on a Police Fulbright Fellowship Award, to study the work of full time School Resource Officers.

According to the Centre for the Prevention of School Violence (CPSV) at North Carolina State University, the concept of placing officers in schools was first seen in the 1950s in Flint Michigan, where the police department had embraced the idea of community policing. During the 1960s and 1970s the programme began to spread across the USA before languishing in the 1980s. It was not until the 1990s that the programme began to gain momentum and develop into the many School Resource Officer (SRO) programmes that now operate across the country.

The role of the SRO includes three main roles:

- Problem solver and liaison to the community
- Educator
- Law enforcement/safety specialist.

## Congressional definition

The US Congressional Definition of a School Resource Officer is 'a career law enforcement officer, with sworn authority, deployed in community-orientated policing, assigned by the employing police department or agency to work in collaboration with schools and community-based organisations'.

His or her duties are to:

1 Address crime and disorder problems, gangs and drug activities affecting or occurring in or around elementary or secondary school

2 Develop or expand crime prevention effort for students

3 Educate likely school-age victims in crime prevention and safety

4 Develop or expand community justice initiatives for students

5 Train students in conflict resolution, restorative justice and crime awareness

6 Assist in the identification of physical changes in the environment that may reduce crime in or around the school

7 Assist in developing school policy that addresses crime and recommend procedural changes.

*Atkinson, A (2000), The Successful School Resource Officer Programme*

## Time spent on roles

Surveys conducted by the CPSV state that the law enforcement role tends to dominate the role of the SRO in schools, which occupies almost 50% of their time; 30% of the time is spent on counselling and advising and 20% is spent on law related education, as can be seen from Figure 2.

It is important to note that the amount of time devoted to each of these roles differs between SROs and the schools in which they operate. My own observations in the USA have revealed that SROs in high schools tend to spend a greater amount of their time dealing with law enforcement, whereas middle school officers often enjoy the luxury of spending more time in the classroom covering lessons on law and developing relationships with children.

**Figure 2  Time spent on SRO Roles**
*Centre for the Prevention of School Violence, Research Bulletin, Volume 1, Number 2, July 1997*

The exact role of the SRO tends to differ between schools and police departments throughout the USA. Attempts to understand these differing roles have been made clearer, thanks to the work of the CPSV which has conducted a number of surveys to discover more about the life of the SRO.

Much of this work has been conducted with the co-operation of the National Association of School Resource Officers, in conjunction with their annual conferences. What is quite apparent from these surveys is that there is no single agreed definition for the role of an SRO.

Such work has enabled researchers to better understand the fundamental principle behind SROs and examine where one stands with reference to our understanding, knowledge and best practices about the approach. Further reading on this subject is contained in one such article: *School Resource Officers: What we know, What we think we know, What we need to know*, CPSV, 2001.

## Programme challenges

In contrast to this uncertainty surrounding the role of the SRO, there is a fundamental agreement that a number of challenges exist which are necessary for the successful implementation of an SRO programme

These challenges include communication, expectations, the SRO programme, the officer and the relationships that the SRO must form.

The following is a list of issues which must be continuously addressed if an SRO programme is to be successful; it has been taken from the Community Orientated Policing Services (COPS) training manual National School Safety Center.

- Developing and maintaining effective communication between and among law enforcement, school officials and the community
- Understanding and communicating that the placement of an SRO in a school does not mean that a school is unsafe
- Understanding that the placement of an SRO in a school does not mean that the staff no longer need to be concerned about school safety
- Paying for an SRO programme
- Facing liability issues which surround SRO programmes
- Addressing 'turf wars' which can arise between different agencies
- Recognising the impact of an SRO programme on the internal workings of involved law enforcement agencies
- Selecting the 'right' SRO for a school
- Selecting and training the SRO supervisor
- Training the SRO to be successful
- Preventing SRO 'burnout'
- Evaluating the SRO's performance
- Developing effective and efficient school assignment and coverage plans
- Making expectations of all involved parties clear and understood
- Understanding the differences between school discipline and criminal law
- Understanding the differences between formal counselling and the kinds of counselling or referral that the SRO will handle
- Creating and maintaining successful working relationships between the SRO and the local law enforcement agencies
- Creating and maintaining successful working relationships between the SRO and community resources
- Creating and maintaining successful relationships between the SRO and the principal and school staff
- Creating and maintaining successful relationships between the SRO and the students
- Determining whether the SRO programme is successful.

## Effectiveness of School Resource Officers

More recently, studies have been conducted to assess the effectiveness of SROs and also to answer the question of whether the deployment of officers in schools (as opposed to performing normal police duties) is worth the money, time and resources expended.

A good example of this type of research to measure SRO effectiveness was conducted by the CPSV in conjunction with a division of the North Carolina Department of Juvenile Justice and Delinquency and Duplin County schools.

Pre-test surveys were conducted on students and teachers or administrators at the schools to provide base line data from which to assess the school climate and impact of the SROs. (CPSV Research Brief No 4, June 2001)

The survey questions focused on school climate issues and their ability to measure behaviours, perceptions, and feelings of students and teachers or administrators with reference to school safety.

In nearly all examples of such research, post-test surveys reveal that the introduction of SROs has been positive, in terms of knowledge, interaction and perceived impact.

## Negative attitudes

Not all schools across the USA are in favour of school-based police officers. In fact, according to an article in *The Guardian Education Supplement* 15 May 2000, 'a school in Brooklyn sent the cops packing'. Brooklyn, a tough neighbourhood of New York, has a reputation for guns and knives being routinely brought into schools; it was this that prompted the state to make it mandatory for schools to have security guards.

### El Puente High School

El Puente is a typical high school in New York; although its principal was averse to the use of security guards, he reluctantly acceded to the request. According to the principal, its success in achieving academic success without violence is that 'we simply love and care for our students.'

The school's approach to dealing with incidents of pupils carrying knives, or perpetrating acts of violence, is to sit them down and talk to them; staff explain that pupils do not need to protect themselves at this school, because it's a safe place. The principal explains that it's only because these pupils are so used to carrying knives to protect themselves that they bring them to school in the first place.

Rather than report an offending pupil to the authorities (which, according to the principal, would be to adopt an approach of zero tolerance) he prefers to focus on the pupil's human rights and to deal with these incidents internally.

It can be argued that the principal is simply providing these pupils with a safe haven, where they know they will not be challenged or prosecuted for carrying a knife – in a country where one in eight teenagers admitted to carrying a weapon to school at least one day a month, and 133,700 violent crimes against teachers were recorded in one year.

## Rich East High School

Not all schools are as radical as the one described above, neither do all schools welcome the idea of having a resident police officer with open arms. There are a large number of schools throughout the US who fit into this 'middle of the road' category, one of which includes Rich East High School, which in 1987 reluctantly introduced the first police/school liaison programme to the area.

The effect that this had on the school is outlined in *Education is everyone's business*, an article by a former principal, Brian J Barry. National School Safety Centre (1995).

The principal states that prior to the project 'We reported little of what could be called violent'. Crimes would be dealt with 'in house' and, adds the principal, 'For the sake of our good image, if the police had legitimate business at the school, they were expected to park in the back lot, out of sight, so no one would infer there was trouble in the building.'

The teachers at this Illinois school wanted to know 'Why do we need police in our buildings?' and a cartoon even appeared in the school newspaper depicting 'inmates and guards under the school house roof'.

However, six years after the scheme had been implemented, the principal explains that 'the front of the school resembled a police station parking lot with the watch commander, the chief of police, the captain, two of our police liaison officers and one of the street officers having lunch with the assistant principal in the faculty lunchroom. By that time our school security program had become entrenched.'

What happened in those years between 1987 and 1993 to cause such a turnaround in people's attitudes? The principal outlines three main things that occurred during that time:

Firstly, there was a realisation by both a police officer and the assistant principal that a 'co-operative effort between the school and the police could produce immense benefits for both organisations'.

Secondly, local police officers convinced the school staff that the security programme was essential to create a safe learning environment and enhance learning for all.

Lastly, the police worked in a variety of ways to convince the school community that the scheme could be successful. The strategies included using their expertise to teach classes in law and social studies, and train pupils how to drive safely. The intention was to prove to the staff that the police could become an integral part of the school.

In addition, those who were involved in the development of the project spent a large proportion of their time 'establishing objectives and subsequently planning for the ultimate co-operative effort between the school and the police department'.

It appears that after reviewing other school/police partnerships that are in operation around the USA, there are a number of other programmes which experience similar stories of success, as well as some problems.

## School Resource Officers' web forum

Many of these problems are described on an Internet forum organised by the CPSV. The articles on the website highlight difficulties experienced by SROs in relation to their work and their relations with differing members of the partnership. For more information see www.cpsv.org

All of the replies offer sound advice for tackling issues, which all the officers seem to have experienced at some stage. It is reassuring to know that problems which officers may encounter are not uncommon – and that there appear to be strategies for overcoming them. Two examples of website postings are shown on the next page.

**Subject: Being left out**

There is a moral issue of belonging. The department I work for SRO's are not accepted by the Sheriff's Dept. We are looked down upon by all other Deputies The Administration doesn't get us the equipment we need to do the job and act like the schools should pay for what we need. The schools don't want us meddling in their issues. They want us to hide away in our offices (if we have one) and not come out unless they need us. They feel like the SO (Sheriff's Office) should supply us our equipment because we are deputies, but if something happens they wonder why we can't take care of the problem.

*SRO Web Forum*

Reply

Chris, You're not alone. I work for an SO that has over 400 deputies. The four SROs are looked upon as 'kiddie cops' by the rank and file. We even have Sgts and Lieutenants that feel we're not real cops unless we are working nights. It makes for a rough tour of duty...As far as the schools go, get into as many classrooms as you can. In a short time the students will warm to you and the school officials will hear a ton of good things about you. Go to as many school events as you can. The more the public sees you, the better they feel...Don't worry too much about the guys humping the calls in your area. When they see how many reports the SROs take care, of they will warm to you. Attend training with the troops so they don't forget who you are. When all else fails a box of donuts can go a long way at a shift briefing. Hang in there. You are making a difference in those kids' lives.

*SRO Web Forum*

---

**Subject: SRO ex-misfit**

I don't want to be the advice guy but wow!!! It is
amazing that we all have the same basic problems.
I cannot wait to go top training on this and possibly
meet more in my boat... The school does not want
to have reports done because it shows what the
kids are really doing. There is so much grey area in
this job.

*SRO Web Forum*

---

## National Association of School Resource Officers survey

One of the training events to which the officer in the reply above refers,
is the annual conference of the National Association of School Resource
Officers (NASRO). In July 2001 at Miami, Florida, where the 11th
annual conference was held, a total of 1,000 surveys were distributed to
SROs in attendance. This represented approximately 10% of NASRO's
7,000 members, and was 'designed to provide the first nationally known
concrete data on SRO demographics, SRO program design and
operations, and SRO program impact and perceptions.' (NASRO School
Resource Officer Survey, 2001)

A brief summary of its findings which are of relevance to this work and
which reveal some of the problems which SROs face across the country
when attempting to implement and develop the school/police programme
are shown below:

- Officers feel that their work improves school safety and prevents
  crime and violence and that they have a positive relationship with
  students, school administrators, teachers, and support personnel.
- However, despite these good links, SROs still believe that school
  crime is underreported to police, although their presence does
  impact on the accuracy of school crime reporting.
- Another area of concern is that, aside from school/faculty staff,
  SROs state that the majority of individuals who influence the
  school (such as the press, elected officials, police officers and,
  notably, researchers and academics) do not understand the roles
  and functions of the SRO.

One can sympathise with the feelings of these officers and agree with the irony that it is the pupils who understand the role of the SRO better than anyone else; regrettably, pupils have no influence in shaping public opinion or determining policy or funding issues about the programme.

Once again, the common source of concern for SROs is the relationship which they share with their principals and the other key players – and how this can adversely affect the success of the programme.

The CPSV has determined that

> 'the relationship between the two parties is of critical importance to the successful implementation of the SRO approach in schools. When built upon communication and co-operation, this relationship can be the cornerstone for secure, safe and orderly schools'.
>
> Center for the Prevention of School Violence, 2001

Their research concludes that the starting point for the principal:SRO relationship is the realisation that the principals and SROs 'share a common vision'. Other findings included the clear defining of roles and a framework for the daily operation of the programme. It also highlights the fact that, although everybody wants the school to be a safe secure learning environment, it is ultimately the school and the principals who can, by mutual communication and co-operation, help make the 'vision a reality'.

# CHAPTER 4

# Partnerships

## Safer schools

The Crime and Disorder Act (1998) requires all local authorities working in partnership with relevant agencies to develop strategies to reduce crime and disorder in their area. DfES guidance (Social Inclusion: Pupil Support, Circular 10/99) sets out principles for pupil inclusion within a statutory framework.

One of these initiatives was the placement of a police officer in school on a permanent basis. This gave rise to the formation of the Safer School Partnership, which was already in the process of being developed by the Youth Justice Board for England and Wales; it provided a focused approach to combat the high levels of crime and antisocial behaviour being committed by and against young children in the school community across the country. The scheme is supported by the Department for Education and Skills, the Home Office, the Youth Justice Board for England and Wales, the Association of Chief Police Officers, the Association of Chief Education Officers, the Secondary Heads' Association and the National Association of Head Teachers.

The scheme sets out specific aims and objectives that act as a guide to the partnership and are the basis of the job description or roles for the police officer in partnership with the school community. These roles are ones that should be built upon existing roles which have been established and developed by schools officers over a number of years; however, the role of the school beat officer is clearly much more proactive that that of the schools liaison officer.

In April 2002, the Prime Minister and Home Secretary announced a series of focused initiatives to reverse the worrying rise in street crime figures, in particular across the ten 'safer cities', which account for 82% of all the robberies that occur in England and Wales.

Within the ten police force areas, a total of 34 local education authorities (LEAs) with the highest levels of truancy and crime are being targeted to implement a package of measures aimed at improving pupil behaviour in schools. According to Safer School Partnership Guidance, 2002, these include, as well as police in schools:

- New or expanded learning support units
- Electronic registration systems to monitor attendance throughout the school day
- Intensive truancy sweeps
- Full-time education for excluded pupils
- Multi-agency behaviour and education support teams (BEST) who can intervene early to prevent bad behaviour and tackle its causes
- A named key worker (who may be part of the BEST team) for every pupil deemed to be at risk
- Activities during school holidays targeted on pupils at risk of criminal behaviour.

---

**Aims of the Safer School Partnership**

To reduce the prevalence of crime and victimisation amongst young people and to reduce the number of incidents and crimes in schools and their wider communities by:

- Working together to provide consistent and appropriate support and intervention to divert young people from social exclusion and criminality.
- Sharing information to identify those young people at risk of becoming victims or offenders as well as those who already are.

To provide a safe and secure school community which enhances the learning environment by:

- Reducing the incidence of bullying and violent behaviour experienced by pupils and staff in school and the wider community.
- Reducing substance misuse in the school and wider community.

- Developing crime prevention strategies to improve the physical security of the school and the personal safety of all who use it.

- Developing a multi-agency approach to supporting teachers and other school staff in managing the learning environment.

To ensure that young people remain in education, actively learning and achieving their full potential by:

- Developing strategies to improve attendance, by addressing both authorised and unauthorised absences

- Supporting vulnerable young people through transition, between phases in their education and other aspects of their lives.

- Raising attainment by ensuring a calm learning environment free from disruption.

To engage young people, challenge unacceptable behaviour, and help them develop a respect for themselves and their community by:

- Developing a whole-school approach to conflict resolution

- Ensuring that young people have opportunities to learn and develop citizenship skills

- Promoting the full participation of all young people in the life of the school and its wider community and decisions that directly affect them.

*Safer School Partnership, 2002*

There are now over 100 school beat officers in the UK and a number of these projects are currently being evaluated by the Youth Justice Board. The formal results of this evaluation are eagerly awaited, but anecdotal evidence following visits to boroughs and conversations with schools officers, teachers and pupils have resulted in some extremely positive feedback, which will be highlighted in the following chapters.

## Developing a partnership

As we have seen, not everybody is keen on the idea of placing police officers in school on a full-time basis; many of the arguments centre on the reluctance to see uniformed officers per se. What must be emphasised is that the role of the school beat officer, as defined by the Safer School Partnership, is merely an extension of the good work that officers have performed over a number of years in schools. The officers are more focused in their approach to young people and their attendance in and around schools is not a new phenomenon.

Their work does differ, however, from the traditional role of classroom-based teaching lessons on subjects such as bullying and drugs, which has been readily accepted by most schools across the country. The challenge is now for schools and police services to see the need and advantages of the new schools beat officer approach and to understand how to develop this relationship.

## Identifying a partnership

Not every school needs a full-time police officer; it may be that the school and the police service feel that, due to its geographical location or its pupil make up, the school manages to function perfectly well without any formal intervention from the police. While it may be true that a school does not suffer from sporadic outbreaks of violence or reports of theft and bullying, that does not mean that the school would not benefit from working in partnership with the police. It is of course, only realistic that the police service can only provide officers for a limited number of schools across the country; those which stand to benefit the most from hosting a full-time officer will be those schools situated within crime 'hotspots'.

For an area to be described as a 'hotspot' will ultimately be defined by police statistics for that region, which reveal the number of recorded crimes. Although it is usually apparent who the victims are, and when and where the crimes occur – as well as the likely suspects – it is essential that the police conduct a thorough statistical analysis of an area in which a school is located, to justify highlighting the area as a crime 'hotspot'. This information obviously becomes good justification to present to a potential school, to explain how they could benefit from a school beat officer.

Another way of gauging the level of crime in a particular region is to understand the urban myths that surround that area, usually based on past crimes and reputations. Many schools are subjected to the stigma of being labelled 'troubled' or 'problematic' purely on anecdotal information. It is here that schools develop reputations which deter parents from sending their children to that school; it is also one of the reasons why heads of schools are reluctant to entertain the idea of a full-time officer, for fear that it may send out a message to the community that the school is unsafe and that the establishment has called in the police as a last resort to 'sort out' pupils who are out of control and beyond the recall of the head.

Police services must guard against approaching schools based on this labelling theory; and schools must be willing to accept that adopting a beat officer does not signal a failing or a weakness. Schools should be seen as safe places, where staff and pupils can work together in safety. It is, for some, a change of culture, in that a police officer's presence often conjures up suspicion or concern that something is awry. In other parts of the world, such as the USA, officers are regularly seen in schools, eating in the canteen with other officers, or walking around the school. It is not uncommon for several marked police vehicles to be seen parked in the school car park or for officers to be present at after-school football games. Parents view this as normal and acceptable and actively encourage such practices, as they feel it sends out the message that the school is a safe school which values its pupils, and that crime will not be tolerated within the school community. Pupils want to go to the school and parents want their children to attend.

I would suggest that, in Britain, the same has not been true in the past, and that many – parents, teachers, and pupils alike – feel that a police presence sends out a different message: one of hostility and danger.

I personally share this concern, but would add that a co-ordinated approach is needed by the police and schools to draw on their own 'in-house' information. For the police, this would be the statistical analysis as outlined above; and for schools, an audit of their own figures on exclusions, truancy and reports of crime within the school.

## Consultation

Once it is identified that a police:school partnership may be desirable, (based on, amongst other things, solid statistical data) then the partnership has to adopt a strategy to advertise this and to make known to the local community what its intentions are – and how this has come about. During the development stages of the Safer School Partnership, many schools expressed concern that they did not wish to attract unwanted national publicity around their partnership with the police as they felt it would be viewed as too radical and attract unwanted criticism. This is certainly a concern for the schools and it is a general theme that has emerged from several of the earlier newspaper reports that covered police working in schools; they frequently centred heavily on the schools being 'problematic' and 'troubled'.

A far safer method is to devise a strategy for informing all the school community and arranging a consultation exercise – not only to outline the essence of the scheme but also to allow those affected to voice an opinion. In this way, everybody has a chance to contribute towards shaping the project and it also provides a useful arena to address serious concerns or challenges that have been overlooked or ignored.

It is important to remember that each school is different; what works in one school in a borough may not necessarily work, a mile down the road, in another. With this in mind, each school needs the opportunity to explore the implications of the Safer School Partnership and draw its own conclusions on what it can offer the school.

A practical way to achieve this is through the medium of a statement issued in the school newsletter, outlining the aims of the scheme and an open evening during which the school and the police can explain the scheme. Several London boroughs have done just this:

**CASE STUDY**

### Hackney

*Officers from the Hackney police division have met with a representative from the LEA along with head teachers from five of the borough's secondary schools. During the meeting they discussed the role of the officers and the general protocol. They identified a head teacher to be part of the interview panel for officer selection and put forward a number of actions, which include a newsletter to publicise the forthcoming role and an evening event. These actions will lend support to the initiative and provide an opportunity for parents, pupils and members of the community to find out for themselves what the prospect of police in schools will entail. Links have also been made with the NSPCC around the deployment of counsellors in schools, with whom the officer can work to support victims of crime. In addition the borough organised a launch at one of the secondary schools, to which the local mayor and MP were invited, along with representatives from the police, education, YJB, Home Office and – most importantly – the pupils.*

### Lambeth

*Officers from Lambeth police division have met with the council's deputy chief executive as well as representatives from partner agencies such as Social Services and Youth. At the meeting was a presentation and discussion around the role of a school-based officer. In addition, police representatives met with the LEA's director of education and the head teachers from the three participating schools to discuss the protocol. Heads were very keen to be part of the officer selection process and requested that an evening road show could be organised to inform the school and its community about the forthcoming proposals.*

This is a period of consultation for all to express an opinion and understand what is happening and allows those interested to help shape the roles of the partnership which will bring clarity and guidance; without this, the scheme will hit difficulties at a later stage.

## Establishing roles and responsibilities

Once all parties with a vested interest in the scheme (parents, pupils, teachers, police, support staff, local community and school governors) have understood the reason for police in schools and have helped form the protocol, then an agreement must be written up and agreed by the head teacher and senior police officer, as well as the school beat officer who will ultimately have to undertake the role.

Contained within this agreement will be issues such as:

- Aims and objectives
- SBO assignment
- Hours
- Chain of command
- Training
- Dress code.

Figure 3 pictures the overall strategic framework for Safer Schools, and provides partners with an understanding of the roles and support network within the partnership. It is essential that all parties understand this concept and can clearly see how their role is an important part of the model and complements the overall structure, as well as adding balance and a holistic approach to the partnership.

**STRATEGIC FRAMEWORK**

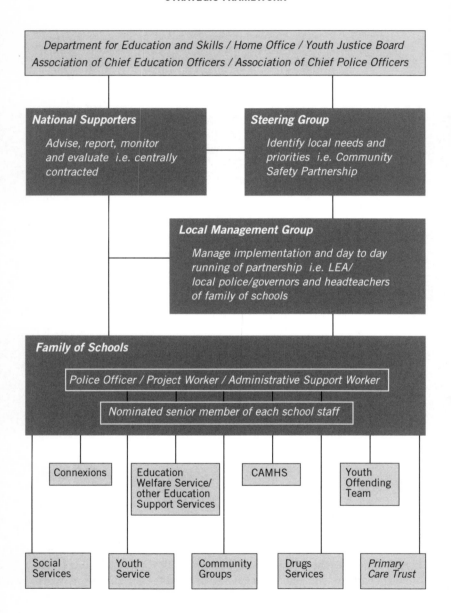

**Figure 3   Strategic Framework**

*Safer Schools Guidance (2002)*

## Agreeing roles and responsibilities

These issues then need to be discussed and agreed, in terms of how they will be performed, overseen or monitored to ensure that the scheme runs smoothly and effectively.

These are some of the main issues which cause most concern – for both the police and the school management – and which thus need to be addressed from the outset, if partnerships are to be successful.

## Hours of duty

One of the incentives for many schools officers is the chance to work sociable hours: traditionally Monday to Friday, between 8am and 4 pm. Some boroughs allow their officers to work extended hours so that they can be there before the start of the school day and are able to stay behind to see the pupils safely home from school and deal with any impending paperwork. These hours of duty need to be agreed at an early stage with the school, so that they are aware of when the officer will be present and able to support them. Of equal importance is to inform the school of when the officer will be away and whether there will be a replacement to cover their duties. Schools can become increasingly demanding in this respect, especially when they have financially invested in the partnership by providing rooms, telephone lines and radios for the officer. On several occasions, schools have expressed concerns that 'their' officer has not been present at the school, even when this has been for laudable reasons such as training. This can of course be seen in a positive light, as school officers become a victim of their own success by becoming an integral part of the school community: the schools value and depend upon them to such a degree that they cannot do without the officer. What is of paramount importance is that there is some formal agreement and notice given that will clearly determine what hours the officer will work.

## Uniform

This is an issue that causes a great deal of debate. Although there are times when a flexible approach is most productive, the role of a schools officer is a uniformed one and requires the officer to be suitably dressed. However, it is certainly a good idea to spend the first few weeks in plain clothes in order to develop relationships with the school community and for them to see the officer as a person – and not to make assumptions about that officer simply because of the uniform. This makes it easier when the officer dons uniform for the first time; everyone is able to know the individual and socialise with them and see beyond the uniform.

The uniform is an effective tool for the officer; for many people this is still a form of authority that people like to see. They view it as a positive image, which represents the police service and acts as a visible deterrent to intruders and as a source of security and comfort.

There will, of course, be some who do not like the uniformed presence of police officers in schools, especially with the array of equipment which officers now have to carry. There are health and safety issues with officers carrying all their equipment within a school and justifiable concerns that these items need to be stored safely when not in use – and in ways which ensure that nothing can be mislaid or acquired by inquisitive children. It is not always necessary to wear uniform; there may be circumstances where officers choose not to be in full uniform, such as after-school events, sports days, school concerts or at the request of the head.

## Chain of command

These issue needs to be clearly defined at an early stage between the head, line managers and the officer. The officer must be included in this scenario as, too often, decisions are made about the officer's role without consulting the officer. Clear guidelines around the chain of command will allow the officer to have a clear understanding of who is responsible for what; who to approach when they have concerns or questions and, ultimately, who is responsible and accountable for which areas. Examples of issues which fit across these areas include the reporting of crime, what will be investigated, hours of duty and job description.

## Supervision

There is also a real need for the school beat officers to have support from their immediate supervisors and also from their own colleagues in the police service. Police supervisors play an important role in maintaining the link for the officer between the world of education and the police service. The role of the school beat officer is first and foremost as that of an officer, although it is easy for this distinction to become blurred and the officer can quickly begin to lose his or her identity. It is very confusing, and at times bewildering, to become immersed in a culture which is entirely different to one's own. Suddenly, one becomes the outsider – a uniform apart from that of the school, an authority figure, respected but often despised; one that is not regarded as a real teacher by the school community and one that is not regarded as a real policeman by many colleagues.

The level of supervision that officers receive as school beat officers is essential to the success of the role. Because of its lack of recognition and confusion about the SSP role by many supervisors, some schools officers have in the past simply been left to undertake their work on their own. This can be of mutual benefit to both parties; officers can get on and perform the role they were asked to and supervisors who invariably have a number of portfolios to manage can leave the experts to do their job. This however is where the problems begin: officers become emerged in a unique role in which they become the specialists over time and which very few other people can understand or sympathise with when issues and problems (inevitably) arise.

This divide is often why schools officers feel undervalued and frustrated. There is no one to turn to and seek advice from when they need it most. This has a spiralling effect, as officers become increasingly detached and isolated in their role and take it upon themselves to deal with any problems.

Those teams of officers who appear to have good team spirit and camaraderie, and who manage to deal successfully with impending issues and concerns, state that this is due in part to good supervision by the supervisors and a good understanding of their roles and impact of their work by senior management who take a vested interest in what they do.

Interestingly, those officers who are most sceptical about the SSP role are often part of a team that is poorly supervised. This throws up the obvious need for supervisors to receive the same training as the school officers, in order to keep up with the changing issues that are emerging from this new role. Supervisors also need to stand up for their officers and ensure that they are supported with the necessary equipment to perform their role. This includes computers, laptops, mobile phones; where possible, they need to be ring-fenced from weekly extractions, which causes resentment by some schools which become too dependent on their new officers.

## Team-based

It is with these points in mind that school officer teams would be more effective if they were housed in one central office as a team and not split up and assigned to different police stations. There is a trade-off here, in that by splitting up the officers they become more interactive with sector teams and help to solve problems within the school community in partnership with their police colleagues, which in turn helps to raise their profile. However, there is a need for them to have their own office and identity as a specialist who can regularly speak and discuss issues with other colleagues – in particular the supervisor – on a daily basis. This is much harder to do when assigned to a sector and, once again, supervision becomes an issue as sector supervisors are rarely familiar with the internal workings of a school and the specific problems which are experienced in this partnership.

School officers who work as a team are much more effective in their jobs; they display more signs of positive attitude towards their roles and are keener to assist their colleagues and take on new ideas. A good way of developing this attitude is to ensure that the officers regularly arrange a breakfast meeting before attending school; they can share ideas and experiences and update each other with useful intelligence and offer encouragement and support.

The benefits of housing the officers under one roof allows them to be supervised more effectively, as the supervisor will better understand the issues affecting the officers and will be able to deal with them sensitively and expeditiously. The benefits of the officers being assigned to sectors include good relationships with the sector teams and close proximity to the schools. These benefits can also arise if the officers take it upon themselves to inform the sector teams of their work: the best way to accomplish this is to invite sector officers into the school. An opportunity to have a cup of tea will attract most officers and this is a great way of informing them of any issues that the officer is concerned about. It also raises the profile of the school officer and, in terms of safety, it allows sector officers to see where their colleagues work and the layout of the schools, should they require assistance.

If officers are based in schools local to their division, they can easily make their way on police bicycles; this increases the visible presence of officers on the street and is a cheap, efficient and effective way of policing the borough. It also deters officers from travelling to and from schools in 'half blues' (i.e. not in full uniform) or plain clothes, as they would not have the full complement of their equipment with them; this can attract criticism from many regular officers, who feel that school officers are only prepared to deal with issues in their school. This can also cause some resentment from sector teams and leads to poor relationships with them: it increases the divide between the two and helps to perpetuate the belief that schools officers are not 'real officers'.

## Reporting of crime and arrests

What constitutes a crime in a school and who will deal with the matter? Is a playground fight a matter for police to deal and treat as a crime – or is it a disciplinary matter for the school to take care of? Is there room for both to intervene or will this cause friction within the partnership? Can officers arrest on site? Do they need the permission of the head or can they use their discretion? There are a number of key issues here, and work is currently underway to give clear guidance on these matters. The YJB, who have consulted with the DfES and Home Office, are to publish some standard form of reporting crime and the way in which it should be dealt with; it is hoped that this will provide a consistent message for schools and a target for police to work towards.

As with all these issues, it is for each individual school and police borough to reach an agreement, or protocol, over the way in which the officer will work. Such a protocol should, where possible, be the same for each school in that borough, as this allows officers who are called to deal with disturbances in a neighbouring school to have an understanding of how they should operate. Youth Justice Board *Crime Recording by Police Officers Working in Schools* (Draft), 2003.

## Communication with head teacher

This cannot be emphasised enough; the relationship developed between the officer and the head is often the mainstay of the partnership. Without the support and good will of the head, the scheme will experience extreme difficulties, which will manifest themselves in a number of ways. To avoid this, officers need to meet regularly with their heads or senior management team, in order to update each other about what has been happening. This will progress the partnership. Over time, relationships will develop and a mutual feeling of trust will follow that will lead to a better understanding of each other's role and a wider scope to achieve partnership work.

It is within these meetings that officers often become aware of the real issues that lie beneath the surface – in particular, the extent of crime that has been reported to the head or the levels of truancy and exclusion. For many officers, the reluctance of heads to report crime is often a major cause of frustration and a stumbling block for the partnership. Heads are understandably reluctant to report all crimes to police – as the police, of course, have a duty to report and investigate them. However, the deliberate cover-up of some serious incidents is not the aim of the partnership and, in light of this, officers need to be able to fall back upon the agreed protocol and highlight the need for such crimes to be reported.

## Opposition

Although already mentioned, there will undoubtedly be opposition from certain members of the public with regard to police officers working in school. What is potentially far more damaging to the partnership, and the officer in particular, is the level of criticism that the officer may receive directly from teaching staff of a certain political standpoint. Although this is an area which is not usually considered in the setting up of protocols, it is an important issue to consider. This is due to the high number of officers who are encountering incidents where a small minority of teachers have passed comments to officers, held trade union meetings or delivered inflammatory literature about the work of the officer.

This can have a devastating effect on the officer, who may find that criticism of this nature within a position (which is at times frustrating and extremely isolated) will become too much to handle. This is, of course, where close supervision and support from the officer's line managers is crucial.

## Selecting school officers

### Kiddie cops

This is based on the premise that officers who work in school do not perform real police work; they are looking for the soft option; they are 'kiddie cops', who are surrogate teachers and avoid the typical 'macho' roles of traditional police work which encompass shift work, arresting 'villains' and driving fast cars.

Whilst such distinctions could, possibly, have been levelled at the work of the school liaison officer the same criteria does not apply to the new school beat officers; this is an area that both the officer and the supervisor need to impress upon other officers. This is imperative for a number of reasons: firstly it is essential that the right type of officer applies for this role: whereas the feeding ground for school liaison officers often consisted of officers on recuperative duties or those approaching their twilight years of service, this new role requires an altogether different calibre of officer. This can be achieved only through educating and informing colleagues of the roles of the officer and encouraging other colleagues to work in partnership with them. Secondly, the qualities required may well be those which officers in the criminal investigation department or territorial support group, for example, possess. Many head teachers are quite specific in the type of police officer that they wish to see employed at the school and, as previously noted, many have asked to be a part of the selection process such that they can assess the qualities of the officers.

## Qualities of a school officer

In a survey of teachers (Briers, 2003), there were a number of qualities that were highlighted which teachers felt school officers should possess in order to work in schools. They included a number of attributes with a real concern and love for children featuring as the most important:

---

**School officer qualities**

| | |
|---|---|
| Ability to work in a team | Intelligence |
| Assertive | Personable |
| Calm | Personality and presence |
| Caring | Politeness |
| Concerned | Professional at all times |
| Consistent | Respectful |
| Co-operative | Self-control |
| Discretion | Sensitive |
| Excellent counselling skills | Strict |
| Empathetic | Supportive |
| Good interpersonal skills | Sympathetic-looking |
| Integrity | Tact |

*Briers 2002*

---

It is these qualities that supervisors need to look for in potential school officers.

In addition, patrol officers in the USA were surveyed and their responses to the question Do you view SROs as real police officers or 'kiddie cops'? were recorded. (Briers, 2003)

- They face the same level of violence as street cops, and they actually deal with more people during a shift than a street cop.
- I view them as a real police officer with additional skills.
- Real police officers. They do a large amount of work for the schools.
- Real police officers – their duties differ from ours only very slightly – their 'beat' is a school.
- Real police – they take care of many issues dealing with juveniles, which leave the beat officers free to respond to other calls.
- I think their statistics for calls handled, reports taken, and arrests made by SROs speak for themselves. They have their hands full.
- Real officers – they get involved in a lot of stuff!!
- Real cops, more experience in those officers.
- They handle all types of crimes in the school.
- Real cops dealing with real issues with juveniles.
- Real police – who have to deal with kids whose parents are totally inadequate.
- Real police officers – they handle similar calls, just at schools.
- I see them as a valuable officer in deployment.

The comments speak for themselves; it is, however, interesting to note that, despite the patrol officers acknowledging and commending the work of the SROs, very few of them said that they would actually want to perform the role. Amongst other reasons stated was the fact that dealing with juveniles was hard work. These officers clearly have a good understanding of the SRO's role and great respect for their work – and in doing so raise the status of the SRO's work. In fact, some police departments regard it as a promotion and award a higher pay scale, whilst for others it is seen as a natural career path for aspiring detectives or promotion.

This is a situation that will change over time in the UK and the respect and esteem in which school officers are held will soon become apparent and help to make it a more attractive proposition for many officers. This is certainly true of SROs in the USA, who have been methodical in their approach to promote the work of the schools officer amongst their colleagues.

## Retention

One of the most important jobs of the supervisor is to actively recruit officers – which is proving to be extremely problematic in many areas. The initial influx of officers to the role was very encouraging, but further recruitment is proving difficult and there are examples of officers making good impressions before moving into new roles, leaving unfilled vacancies.

Supervisors need to look at innovative ways of encouraging officers to take up the post, whilst ensuring that they have the necessary skills and qualities to undertake the role.

## Incentives for officers include:

- Flexible working hours (10-hour shifts), which leaves officers with the school holidays free
- Monday to Friday
- Continuous training
- Additional skills
- Priority payments
- Mentors.

On the next page is a job description and person specification for Safer Schools Officers, as published by the Safer School Partnership (2002). These are only a guide and variations can be made to reflect a schools officer post in a particular area.

DESIGNATED SAFER SCHOOL PARTNERSHIP: YJB/ACPO MODEL

*JOB DESCRIPTION*

**SCHOOL-BASED POLICE OFFICER**

**RANK:**        CONSTABLE

**LOCATION:**    *SCHOOL NAME*

**TENURE:**

**ROLE PROFILE**

The dedicated school-based police officer will be attached to, and based full time, at a designated family or cluster of schools within the Safer School Partnership.

The role will be demanding and varied. It will be focused on working in partnership with the LEA, school staff, education services and agencies to prevent offending and to create a safer school environment. The role will involve a high level of multi-agency working and co-ordination in relation to responses to individual 'high risk' offenders and vulnerable young people when problem solving in the school / community environment.

Core responsibilities will include

1  Working with school staff and others to create and maintain a safe school environment

2  Preventing offending by young people through working with individuals, and through the joint development of programmes within the school community

3  Undertaking targeted PHSE and citizenship inputs as appropriate, and agreed by the school management, thereby contributing to the school learning environment

4  Ensuring that the preventative work within the school is linked to the broader work in the local community undertaken by the Youth Offending Team and Crime and Disorder Reduction Partnership. (This may often be done through existing links co-ordinated by Connexions.)

5    Providing a visible and accessible policing presence within the school setting and its wider community, in accordance with the agreements between the LEA and police for Safer School Partnerships.

The duties required of this role will comprise:

1    Collating detailed data to enable the school(s) to conduct an effective audit of crime, antisocial behaviour, victimisation and fear within its community

2    Investigating crime and dealing with offences from a base in the school setting

3    Becoming involved in analysing crime and incident trends

4    Identifying and working with those young people at high risk of becoming involved (or further involved) in offending behaviour.

5    Motivating and relating well with young people, in particular those identified as at high risk

6    Working with schools towards improving young people's understanding of personal and social issues such as the consequences of crime and misuse of drugs, associated life skills / good citizenship

7    Arranging, and supervising the delivery of, intervention work such as leisure activities, to develop and encourage young people, particularly those at risk of offending or re-offending

8    Linking programme / project work within the school community directly into that of the LEA, local Crime and Disorder Partnership and Youth Offending Team and Connexions

9    Assisting the school in developing whole-school approaches to behaviour management and conflict resolution, such as through restorative justice, conferencing and peer support / mentoring schemes

10   Being involved with the school and Education Welfare service in instigating joint truancy patrols; referring onto the Connexions Personal Adviser where appropriate

11   Focusing specifically on offences of violence and developing appropriate programme responses

12   Contributing to school policy concerning drug-related incidents and accompanying school safety plans

13 Working with staff to agree and prepare appropriate learning materials and delivering appropriate targeted classroom inputs, as agreed with school management

14 Delivering appropriate and targeted classroom inputs, as agreed with school management

15 Developing processes with school staff to ensure children are aware of the pressures they may face during periods of transition, notably from primary to secondary school, but also changes of school, return to school from a period of exclusion or time spent in a young offender's unit

16 Where appropriate being involved in patrolling the routes to and from school(s) to prevent crime and increase the feeling of personal safety

17 Providing community reassurance particularly focusing on the local community and parents/carers of pupils.

## DESIGNATED SAFER SCHOOL PARTNERSHIP: YJB/ACPO MODEL

### *PERSON SPECIFICATION*

### SCHOOL-BASED POLICE OFFICER

(Note – 'E' stands for 'essential')

1   Must possess good interpersonal skills and relate well with others in a team and engage positively with other agencies. (E)

2   Must be committed to equal opportunities and possess a positive and sensitive approach to police/community relations. (E)

3   Must be able to maintain professional and ethical standards internally and externally at all times, particularly providing a positive role model to the younger generation. (E)

4   Must be able to display good potential to develop teaching/presentational skills, particularly to young people of varying age groups, creating a positive impact and holding the attention of the listener. (E)

5   Must be able to maintain good communication skills in both written and oral form. (E)

6   Must be able to display good potential to interact positively and sensitively with young people, particularly those at risk of offending. (E)

7   Must be able to display good potential to understand the school context and how to operate effectively within that. (E)

8   Must be able to understand factors and issues that lead to offending. (E)

9   Must be able to use sound judgement and discretion, utilising experience and knowledge to good effect and be able to identify potential problems. (E)

10  Must be able to collate and identify common threads / pertinent facts from a large amount of information from a variety of sources and then be able to draw well-reasoned conclusions / make recommendations. (E)

11  Must be able to show high levels of interest in community safety matters and be sufficiently creative and self-motivated to generate

work and organise present and future tasks without close supervision. (E)

12 Must be able to devise and implement innovative improvements, adding value to the schools programme and community safety partnerships at local level. (E)

13 Must be able to use own vehicle for police business use, ensuring it is insured for business use. (E)

14 Must be able to display potential to update/maintain computer-based files/indices. (E)

## Training

It is imperative that schools officers receive training around their new roles and responsibilities. There has, to date, been training available through the Youth Justice Board, which has provided potential school officers with the necessary skills to help forge partnerships with schools and develop the Safer Schools Model. Inevitably with all new roles, further training is required as officers face new dilemmas and encounter situations that they feel unable to deal with professionally. In response to this a training manual has been developed by the author to assist officers with their roles; it is explained in the next chapter. It is based on a modular programme and is intended for police officers and partners – who include teachers, support assistants such as Connexions, youth service, drug workers, educational welfare officers and volunteers as well as parents.

## Evaluation

As with all new schemes, there is a real need for them to be evaluated – whether internally or independently. The YJB is currently evaluating four pilot Safer Schools sites across the country; many other partnerships have taken it upon themselves to undertake their own evaluations. These evaluations have generally been done in three different ways:

- **Schools** have endeavoured to look at the rates of truancy and exclusion since the inception of the officer and have relied heavily on anecdotal evidence from pupils and staff about the feeling of security experienced and fear of crime
- Many **police services** have focused on the number of crimes being reported, although a rise in reported crimes can also indicate a willingness by pupils to report crime because they are better supported by the police and have greater confidence in them – and because the opportunity of reporting the crime is now easier
- Some **boroughs** have recorded the number of incidents in the schools that required police assistance and have then compared this to the number of hours saved by not having police officers (usually in a patrol car) attending the school and dealing with them. The effect is that patrol officers are freed up to perform other duties, and school officers – who are arguably better equipped to deal with such incidents – can provide a quicker and more efficient service.

There is an urgent need for many aspects to be properly and consistently evaluated; this will highlight much of the good work that is being undertaken by these partnerships, the positive results of which could influence further investment in the programme. Below is an overview of how the SSP programme could be assessed, by studying four areas: evaluation, environment, efficiency and effectiveness.

If this approach to evaluation is adopted, nationally, across the police services then there will be continuity in the way in which we track the progress of our school officers and their impact upon school communities in accordance with relevant Youth Strategy and SSP guidance.

The impacts of the SSP programme can be identified by studying four areas: evaluation, environment, efficiency and effectiveness. (Center for the Prevention of School Violence, 1997)

- **Evaluation:** This entails conducting baseline measurements on areas such as school violence before embarking upon an SSP programme and then collecting and tracking the data at set intervals throughout the programme. This could include reviewing the number of crimes in the school community, the number of victims, levels of truancy and exclusion and the number of complaints from the local community.

- **Environment:** This involves looking at the impact that the SSP has on the school environment, particularly in terms of the feelings of school safety, attitudes, and behaviours of pupils, teachers and staff. This would be in the form of a survey and could be conducted, by the school officers, on a periodic basis to all members of the school community in order to monitor the success of the scheme.

- **Efficiency:** This looks at how the officers' deployment can seen as being placed 'where the action is' and how their work can be associated with savings for the police service. Are officers deployed in hotspot areas and are their cost savings associated with fewer calls to the control room and sector officers attending the school?

- **Effectiveness:** How well do the officers fulfil their roles? What is the effect they have on incidents such as school violence, both in the schools and the local community?

In addition to this, a generic 'return of work' needs to be compiled by all schools officers. These can be collated to see the volume and diversity of the officer's work and the impact that this is having upon crime levels. It will also reveal training requirements for the officers and a better understanding of what our officers do – and therefore help formulate a job description, which at present is still evolving.

A 'return of work' could include the number of:

- Arrests
- Intelligence reports
- Stop slips (i.e. the number of people stopped for questioning)
- Restorative justice conferences (the number of conferences which have taken place; see Chapter 5, 'Joint training', for more information)
- Meetings
- Diversion schemes
- Patrols
- Crime reports
- Problem-solving 302 Forms (The number of problem-solving processes undertaken. For more information see Chapter 5, 'Problem solving')
- Truancy sweeps
- Meetings attended
- Conferences.

A very effective way of conducting an initial evaluation is for officers, when joining a new school, to undertake a school safety survey with the teachers, pupils, parents and the local community. The survey would focus on any concerns that they had about the school, the levels and fears of crime, and what they expected from their officer.

The survey would be very simple to administer and could be repeated six months into the programme to compare against the findings from the original survey. This would provide valuable information into how the programme had developed and what areas of concern still existed.

## Example of staff survey

Here are some typical questions, adapted from a survey developed in 2000 at Poudre School District, Colorado, USA. Attitude responses would normally be marked on a scale from, say, 0 (very low/never/negative) to 5 (very high/always/positive). Note that a six-point scale forces respondents not to 'sit on the fence', as they cannot choose a middle option; it forces them to edge a fraction towards the negative (if they choose '2') or to the positive (if they choose '3')

1    I am concerned about pupil personal safety at school

2    I am concerned about pupils' personal belongings being stolen or vandalised at school

3    I am aware of the SSP

4    I understand the role of the police officer in school

5    I believe pupils' personal safety at the school will increase because of the presence of the police officer at school

6    In time of need, I would contact a police officer regarding a student's personal problems

7    In time of need I would contact a police officer regarding persons breaking the law

8    I feel that the laws which deal with youth are fair

9    I believe that the police officer in my school is a positive member of the school community

10   I approve of the concept of a police officer participating in school security issues

11   I approve of the concept of a police officer participating in classroom presentations

12   I approve of the concept of a police officer participating in after-school activities

13   All things considered I approve of the concept of having a police officer in my school

*I have had personal contact with my school's officer to:*

14   ... discuss a student at my request

15   ... investigate offences at school

16   ... handle disruptive students

> *For each item select the word which best describes your feelings towards the school officer*
>
> 17  Respect              Disrespect
>
> 18  Like                 Dislike
>
> 19  Comfortable          Intimidated
>
> 20  I have heard comments about the school officer partnership from other parents, community members, staff or students.
>
> *Research and Development Centre, 2000*

## Understanding and familiarisation of the school setting

### Starting in the school

Once a school has been identified and a protocol established between the partnership, police officers need to familiarise themselves with the school setting, which entails understanding the structure of schools and how they operate in practice.

There are four aspects to this, which will require some investigation by the officers if they are to understand and appreciate the protocols of the school:

- They need to learn about the school's policies on issues such as bullying, drugs, truancy and exclusions, as well as having a working knowledge of the National Curriculum with particular reference to Personal, Social and Health Education (PSHE).

- It would be useful for officers to understand how schools develop policies and who is responsible for them. Included in this would be the role of parents, parent governors and parent associations, who are an integral part of the school framework – and are very influential in shaping the school's ethos

- Officers should be aware of their partners' roles and know how to interact with them. These partners would include school support staff such as youth workers, Connexions staff, educational welfare officers, school nurses and drug referral officers

- In addition, officers must know how to interact with the school's pupils and look for ways in which to communicate with them through relevant youth forums or advisory groups.

The most effective way to become established in a school community is to get involved and let others know what your roles and responsibilities are. The more discussions that one has with the school community, and the more that one learns about the school community, the easier it will be to become familiar and established within it.

Strategies to ensure that this happens include publicising the role as much as possible through assemblies or posters that outline the role, and ensuring that one is invited to meetings and events so that others quickly view the officer as 'one of them' and become familiar with the sight of a uniformed police officer. In an ideal situation, the officer should try to secure a base near to the main corridor, by the staff room or the head teacher's office, so that they are aware of what is happening in the school and one that places them in a position to help out quickly if needed.

It is imperative that officers not only familiarise themselves with the roles of the people within the school but also with the physical layout: where are the exits and entrances to the school? This is expanded upon in the next chapter, which explains the roles of the school beat officer in more detail and the importance of such precautions and safety issues.

**CHAPTER 5**

# Roles of the school officer

## Introduction

What is emerging from all this evidence is that there is a need to provide some clear direction for boroughs on the roles of school officers within the framework of the Safer School Partnership (SSP) and local police force youth strategy incorporating the aims and objectives contained within. This could be best achieved by providing all officers with a modular programme of training, which covers four roles and ties in with the national policing model:

- Law
- Educator
- Adviser
- Role model.

Figure 4 (overleaf) describes these roles.

This model encompasses the four roles of the school officer; under each heading there are listed a number of practical roles which form the functions of the job and provide a job description for the officers.

Each role is also coded to indicate where it fits into the six core elements of the National Policing Model: investigation, intelligence, diversion, targeting, problem solving and forensics. There is, of course, an overlap with many of the roles, which may fit into a number of the categories shown.

## Youth crime reduction strategy

It is worth noting that the Home Secretary instigated the setting up, in London, of a Youth Crime Task Force. This brought together policy

## Suggested Skills, Roles and Responsibilities

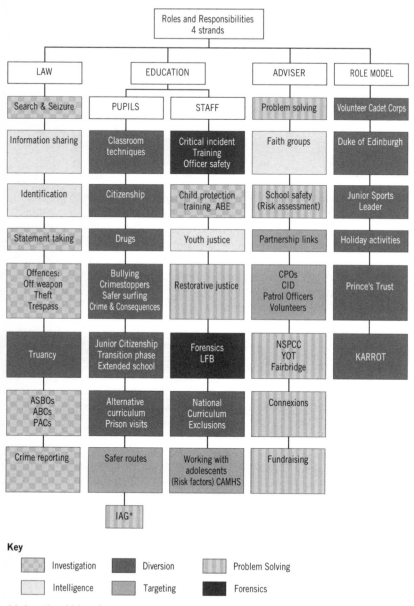

**Key**

| | | |
|---|---|---|
| Investigation | Diversion | Problem Solving |
| Intelligence | Targeting | Forensics |

\* Independent Advisory Groups

**Figure 4  Roles of a School Officer**

makers and practitioners from across the capital, to identify what was working well to reduce youth crime and, more importantly, to determine what else needed to be done. Its work centred on eight key strands namely; education, health, local authorities, police, probation, social services, youth justice and the voluntary/private sector.

It soon became apparent that, by concentrating resources and time in certain areas, significant gains could be made in a short space of time; these nine areas became priority actions for the Task Force:

- Antisocial behaviour
- Behaviour improvement programmes
- CAMHS
- Connexions
- Drug and alcohol provision
- Early years intervention
- Education provision for excluded children
- Extended schools
- Youth inclusion programmes

London Youth Crime Management Board, 2002

All of the above priority areas have been included within the four key roles of the schools officer and, where appropriate, officers are able to contribute to the work of the Task Force and assist with the reduction of offending by young people.

## The four roles

The four roles, which provide the basis for a job description for SSP officers, are briefly introduced and then dealt with in much greater detail a little later in the chapter.

### Law

This role entails providing officers with a body of knowledge around the laws in relation to dealing with pupils on school premises, and how to carry out their duties in response to incidents of crime and antisocial behaviour. Topics covered include powers of search, powers of arrest, educational laws, identification procedures, and the use of Acceptable Behaviour Contracts.

## Education

This role is split into:

- Educational inputs for pupils in the classroom setting, around the key areas of citizenship; they include visits to prisons or suggestions on safer routes to school for the pupils
- Educating the officers and their educational colleagues, identified here as 'joint training', in areas of child protection, critical incident training, officer safety and forensic opportunities; in addition, there is a need to learn how to deal with disruptive pupils and consider some of the reasons which trigger such behaviours.

## Adviser

This role focuses on the officer acting in an advisory role to the pupils (and also to members of staff) when dealing with some of the issues they face as part of a school community. There is a very important role to undertake with partnership agencies such as Youth Offender Teams (YOT), and Connexions, along with other colleagues and professionals within the police service and wider youth justice field.

## Role model

This is a role which should not be overlooked. It plays an important part in building relationships between police and young people by helping them become better citizens and participate more fully in school and the wider community.

## Law

There is a training need for schools officers in relation to those laws which are specific to the school environment. These include laws that are commonly broken by young people such as acts of violence, petty theft, vandalism, and robbery as well as laws of trespass, which are specific to that school. There is also a requirement for officers to understand how laws pertaining to areas of stop and search and the identification and detention of suspects may be affected whilst working in the school community.

## Offences

One of the most helpful documents available, covering laws relating to the school environment, is School security: Dealing with troublemakers which offers guidance for police and schools in the wake of the murder of the London head teacher Philip Lawrence, in December 1995.

There are a number of offences which can be committed (by pupils and staff or other people) on the school premises, such as trespass, assaults, harassment, public order offences, nuisance and disturbance on school premises, possession of offensive weapons, as well as theft, criminal damage and drug-related incidents.

It is important for school officers to become familiar with the finer points of the education-specific laws, as well as other issues such as restraining pupils, the removal of truants and the power to enter schools to search for weapons. For example, under s16 of the Crime and Disorder Act, police officers may remove truants from a public place and return them to school or a place of safety. However, the legislation contains specific controls relating to the scope of the right – i.e. within school hours and when authorised by their police commander and local authority – and it is of course crucial school officers are fully aware of such detail.

## Crime recording

Officers should look at ways of recording incidents that occur in school; they should have structures in place that allow the schools to report crime to police where appropriate. The word 'appropriate' is paramount to the success of such a partnership and, although it is expected that schools will report incidents of a serious nature that require police intervention, it will not be in the interests of anyone – in particular young people – if all crime of a petty nature (as deemed by the school) is relayed to police.

However, for the school's officer to record all such occurrences is good practice, in case of repeated offences by an individual or where similar behaviours become persistent and reveal a pattern of offending.

The previously-mentioned publication, *School security: Dealing with troublemakers*, has a useful form to help school record crime, but note that it will normally be a decision for the police officer in partnership with the school as to what it regards as a minor or major incident.

The form could include information on:

- The types of offences the form is used for
- Details of the reporting staff and of the victim, assailant and any witnesses
- Details of the incident including location, type and any other details

- Outcome
- Any additional information.

To help in this process, draft guidance has been issued around national crime recording standards for police officers working in schools, by ACPO, DfES and the Home Office. Although it is imperative that police and schools agree a format for recording crimes in schools, each case should be looked at on an individual basis and factors should be considered when deciding when to record a crime. For example, in the case of violence by a child or young person on another, we may want to consider factors such as:

- Wishes of the victim
- Aggravating features – for example, racial or homophobic bullying
- Severity of injury sustained/nature of threat received by the victim
- Probability of a repeat incident
- Previous relationship between victim and offender
- Potential impact on the child or young person following any formal police involvement
- Effectiveness of police action/court proceedings
- Future best interests of both parties
- Message sent to other children
- Availability of other courses of action (e.g. restorative justice with consent of victim, or use of Acceptable Behaviour Contracts)

*Crime recording by police officers working in schools* (Draft), 2003

It should also be noted that police should not normally record as a crime any incident they witness on school premises unless either requested to do so by the school or other party, or where it is deemed by the officer to be so serious as to be necessary, even without the school's agreement. For this to be effective there need to be good relations between the police and the school, a theme which runs throughout this book. Without this understanding the partnership will not be able to function and the opportunity to discuss issues such as crime recording and arrests will be lost. What is fundamental to such partnership work is the need to have discretion; it appears, from the formation of the crime reporting standards for schools, that such discretion has been catered for and should lead to continuity for crime recording in schools.

To aid education staff and police in their decision-making, there are a number of useful references or publications to assist with the recording of crime in schools.

- *School security: Dealing with troublemakers, Home Office,* 1997
- *A Legal Toolkit for Schools,* 2002
- *Social Inclusion: pupil support,* 1999
- *Bullying: don't suffer in silence,* 2002.

## Hidden crimes

Schools have, in the past, been understandably reluctant to report crimes to police forces for a number of reasons. Often these have centred on attracting unnecessary publicity but also a belief that such occurrences can be dealt with best within the school environment. Since the arrival of police in schools in the form of the Safer School Partnerships, many officers have explained that they are aware of a number of crimes that go unreported but which are of a serious nature. Approaches to the head and senior management have, often, not resulted in a resolution to these matters; relationships have often deteriorated as a result of a head's reluctance to report and the officer's insistence that they should.

The guidelines are quite clear in so far as schools should make a record of all such incidents and, where appropriate, inform police of such instances. The problem lies in what the school deem as 'appropriate' and it is forthcoming guidance from the Home Office National Crime Recording Sub Group (NCRSG) that will allow this process to take place.

Such concerns on crime reporting are shared the world over; a pilot study of principals and police in Australia reveals the varying problems that exist in terms of attitudes and perceptions when recording crime. The study comprised a set of questions that incorporated scenarios about incidents of vandalism and theft that had occurred in a school and asked for principals to comment on their subsequent course of action. (Challinger)

The study was extremely revealing and the responses varied greatly from suspending pupils to calling the police and offering words of advice. The principals applied their own set of factors that predetermined their course of action. These included whether the child was capable of paying to repair the damage or whether the property damaged or stolen was of high value or significance. Other factors include the age and background of the pupil involved and opinions of staff. What was clear was the lack of any consistent protocol for recording crimes and a general consensus that only in serious incidents would the school notify the police – despite the obvious assistance and support that the police could offer in terms of advice and prevention, as well as intervention.

These scenarios will reflect the experiences of a number of current school officers, so the implementation of a new crime reporting procedure should offer clear guidelines for all parties and negate the need for awkward and obstructive discussion between partner agencies.

In many states in America, schools officials are required by law to report crimes ranging from felonies, misdemeanours to the police, as well as any incidents that involve offensive weapons including firearms. This may include incidents which occur after school on the way home or at specific sporting events or school functions. Conversely, some states require the police to notify the schools of all young people arrested or convicted who attend the school; strict timelines are applied in many cases.

The following table, taken from the Lakewood Police School Office work returns schedule, shows the School Resource Officer activity for the school year August 2000 to May 2001. It includes all incidents reported to full-time schools police officers for four high schools and three 'alternative' high schools (broadly equivalent to our Pupil Referral Units).

| | Aug | Sep | Oct | Nov | Dec | Jan | Feb | Mar | Apr | May | YTD | Prev. YTD |
|---|---|---|---|---|---|---|---|---|---|---|---|---|
| Misdemeanor arrests | 14 | 44 | 33 | 28 | 13 | 22 | 17 | 16 | 21 | 17 | 225 | 209 |
| Misdemeanor reports | 10 | 23 | 26 | 24 | 18 | 26 | 18 | 31 | 20 | 32 | 228 | 242 |
| Felony arrests | 1 | 4 | 0 | 4 | 0 | 8 | 4 | 2 | 2 | 2 | 27 | 11 |
| Felony reports | 7 | 8 | 6 | 7 | 4 | 4 | 7 | 9 | 7 | 9 | 68 | 47 |
| Non-crime reports | 24 | 25 | 25 | 15 | 17 | 24 | 28 | 26 | 25 | 18 | 227 | 326 |
| Student counseling | 87 | 94 | 87 | 110 | 68 | 100 | 97 | 105 | 134 | 140 | 1022 | 973 |
| Parking/traffic summons | 4 | 10 | 10 | 2 | 6 | 4 | 4 | 7 | 5 | 3 | 55 | N/A |

**Table 1: Officer activity**

*International Journal of Police Science and Management, 2003*

## Other methods of crime reporting

Crime committed against young people is under-reported in the UK and victims are often reluctant to report these crimes; this may be due to a number of factors, including peer pressure (in that the child making the report may be seen as 'snitching') or that the crimes themselves are not worth reporting but merely 'part of everyday life'. Often there is concern that the police will not be able to do anything about the matter or take it seriously in the first place; and there is a real fear of retaliation from those who committed the crime. According to the Howard League (2002) only 17% of young people who had become victims of crime stated that they had reported the crime to police.

The school officer has to find ways of making it easier for pupils to report crime in an environment where they feel safe and secure. It is clearly not the job of the officer to 'trawl' for crimes in schools, but instead to be available for pupils to approach and discuss issues with them, which may result in a crime report.

Pupils are often unaware of just how to report a crime and so it is, therefore, imperative that school officers are able to improve reporting procedures for young people. This can be achieved by making reporting easier for young people, more widely available and in a friendly, non-threatening environment. Schools officers have implemented several schemes in an effort to achieve this, including text messaging, 'third party' reporting and use of the Internet.

### Text messaging

In Newham, London, there is a project that aims to increase the confidence of young people in secondary schools in reporting crime – especially street crime and bullying. The pupils are encouraged to use a freetext number to report crime – anonymously, if they wish. The messages are received by members of the local YOT team, who can then liaise with the victims and give them advice and the confidence and assurance about reporting the crime. The service is quick and easy to use and appeals to many young people who may not usually report crime.

### Third party

This initiative aims to improve the level of reporting for hate crimes (generally, racist or homophobic) in the London borough of Lewisham, for young people as well as the rest of the community through independent third-party reporting sites. There are, at present, in excess of thirteen different non-police sites in the borough. Third-party reporting forms were created and suitable people trained in taking the reports.

Initially, the idea was piloted at the local victim support centre in Lewisham, but there are plans to extend the scheme to local secondary schools and colleges as well as a one-stop shop.

## Internet

There are also opportunities for young people to log onto the Internet and report crime via email. This form of reporting has been encouraged since the concerns that have been raised over the number of young people being subject to 'grooming' offences on the Internet.

## Homophobia

In Lambeth, London, and with the assistance of outside agencies, school officers have undertaken classroom sessions with pupils in secondary schools to help educate pupils around issues of homophobia. They explain that the use of homophobic language is a crime; they try to raise the awareness amongst children of how to deal with such issues and how to report the crime. For many young people, being bullied by others – in particular at school – can lead to the victims feeling very distressed. In some cases this can cause them to truant. Bullied victims are often subject to low attainment and increasingly there are reports of them becoming victims of alcohol and drug abuse as well as pregnancy, self-harm and suicide.

## Truancy

A 1999 Department for Education and Employment study found that 'young people who truanted were less likely to be in full-time education, less likely to have a full-time job offering training, and more likely to be unemployed or inactive, than those who had not truanted'. (DfEE, *Tackling truancy together: a strategy document*, 1999)

The problem of truancy is not a new one and recent surveys suggest that things are getting worse with at least 50,000 pupils absent from school on any one day.

The government has acknowledged that truancy is a serious problem and has outlined their intentions to tackle the issue through a variety of schemes and programmes, which provide money and support for local authorities and, more specifically, schools.

School officers have an important role to play in the area of truancy, which affects every school in the country. Section 16 of the Crime and Disorder Act 1988, now gives the police new powers to deal with young people who play truant from school. In partnership with the DfES, police conduct regular truancy sweeps with members of the educational welfare office. They pick up truants and return them to school – by force if necessary.

There are some concerns by schools officers (who are invariably the most suitable officers to undertake these sweeps) that truancy often occurs when pupils are taking exams or are on study leave which makes the process very difficult to enforce; it often leads to confrontations with young people, legitimately not in school, who resent being stopped in the street.

There can also be a problem when these pupils are returned to school, often in small groups, when officers find that the school is not able to deal with the truants in a suitable manner. On occasions these pupils have merely walked straight back out of the school.

To resolve this problem, some school officers – with the educational welfare officer – have begun to conduct regular home visits to the most prolific truants; by concentrating their efforts on the worst offenders they have seen a dramatic turn around in attendance by these pupils.

## Antisocial behaviour

**CASE STUDY**

*In the London Borough of Islington tough new measures have been taken to curb antisocial behaviour amongst teenagers on the local council estates in the form of Acceptable Behaviour Contracts (ABCs) and Parental Control Agreements (PCAs). This has been a joint initiative by both the police and local council under the banner of the Islington Crime Reduction Partnership.*

*They are, in essence, contracts or written agreements between a young person and their parent/guardian, along with the local housing office and police, which specifies that the individual child will not act in such a way that could be recognised as antisocial behaviour. The consequences of failing to abide by the terms, which are formally laid out in an agreement between the parties, can result in legal action – including the loss of tenancy for the family. It has proved to be a very effective tool for educating parents and their children, and empowering them to take responsibility for their antisocial behaviour. The first contract was agreed in November 1999; since then over 100 contracts have been agreed across the borough.*

The success of this work has led to the concept of ABCs being adapted to tackle other areas of concern, such as noise nuisance, and notably the behaviour of young people in secondary schools. It is, potentially, a good way of working in partnership with the school and local authority to assist young people with their challenging behaviour.

Below is an example of how the Islington Antisocial Behaviour Team dealt with an incident on a local housing estate:

**CASE STUDY**

*Issue: A young person was entering a housing association estate and continually damaging property, smoking and drinking until the early hours, and abusing a number of vulnerable residents.*

*Approach: Police and housing staff held an ABC meeting with the young person and his mother. It became apparent that he was not aware of the effect of his behaviour on others and his mother was unaware of his actions. Through discussions at the meeting the underlying cause of the problem was identified: due to lack of space in the family accommodation, the mother was asking her son to leave the property at night. An ABC was signed by the young person and the lead agencies. In addition, the housing officer placed the family on the priority-housing list for more suitable accommodation – on the condition that the son kept to the terms of the contract.*

*Outcome: The family were moved during the six-month period of the ABC. Since signing the contract the young man has not come to the attention of the police or housing staff.*

*Paul Dunn, Islington Antisocial Behaviour Team*
*Home Office, 2003*

Some police officers based in schools have seized upon this initiative and have, in partnership with their school, drawn up their own ABC, which they use to good effect on pupils who have difficulty engaging in school life. A number of them have been issued for pupils who are disruptive and aggressive in school and they have been an effective way of addressing a child's behaviour without resorting to exclusion.

This is, naturally, a very useful tool for both schools and police to tackle antisocial behaviour in school: it enables the pupil to reflect on their behaviour and take steps to ensure that they do not reoffend.

Opposite is an example of an Acceptable Behaviour Contract used in a school in North London, devised in partnership between the police and the school.

## Acceptable Behaviour Contract

Students and Staff at this school are committed to maintaining a safe school community, free from abuse, distress and violence. The police and local authority are working with the school where necessary to help with this. Where students have presented a serious breach of the schools Code for Learning and have demonstrated behaviour that challenges the safety of the school community and its positive learning environment, they place themselves at serious risk of exclusion from the school. As a part of their Pastoral Support Plan, which is designed to help the student make the positive choices necessary to stay at this school, an Acceptable Behaviour Contract is agreed between the student, school, parents/carers and the police.

This contract is made on (date) _____

Between

And (name)

Date of Birth _____

Address _____

_____

I. (name) _____ agree the following regarding
my future behaviour.

1. I will not

2. I will not

3. I will

4. I will

5. I will

I understand that if I do anything which breaks the terms of this contract the school may take further action against me.

Student _____ Print name

Parent/ Guardian _____ Print name

School Representative _____ Print name

Police Officer _____ Print name

Review Date_____

In Laisterdyke High School in Bradford, the head teacher was experiencing a number of incidents within her school, which she described as 'low-level disruption'. As these incidents became more frequent and more serious in their nature, she was only left with the option of exclusion for the offenders, which she felt was not a viable solution to the problem.

It was only after talking to her local police officer that she discovered the term 'School ASBOs', (Antisocial Behaviour Orders). The head teacher set about exploring these, and before long she had organised a meeting with a number of her pupils and their parents, the local police officer and the local authority. 'Of the nine individuals that signed contracts', explains the head teacher, 'one has totally reformed, seven are now operating within the bounds of acceptable behaviour, while one is still playing around with drugs outside school.'

The success of this spread to other nearby schools, which soon experienced similar positive results. As one head teacher explained, 'It is all based on parents being responsible for the behaviour of the kids.'

More information on this subject is available on the Home Office crime and disorder website *www.homeoffice.gov.uk/cdact/asboapg.htm.* or *Paul.dunn2@met.police.uk*

## Education

The second role of the schools officer is that of educator and is an important part of a police officer's interaction with the school community.

### The National Curriculum

Most schools officers in the past would have attended a week-long training course at a local educational college, designed to advise them how to give presentations in class and the use of visual aids. While this is still a useful tool for many school officers, there is also a need for them to understand more about the framework of schools. Many school officers – indeed, many police officers – are competent at delivering presentations and devising lesson plans, bearing in mind most of the material used by school officers has already been produced by outside agencies and a wealth of ideas and lessons are available on numerous websites.

What is thus of at least equal importance for that officers based in schools is a need to understand more about how schools work, who is in charge, the role of school governors and the development of school policies such as bullying and exclusions.

All of these questions will help a school officer fit into a school and have a clear understanding as to how a school is run and where they can contribute most effectively to a safer school.

## Citizenship

Citizenship has traditionally been at the heart of police/school partnerships, with police officers providing educational inputs focusing on pupils' behaviour and their social responsibilities to society. Although the role of police in schools is clearly much wider than before, the need to provide educational inputs encompassed under the umbrella of citizenship is now an important part of the National Curriculum and an essential part of the school officer's inventory of knowledge.

Lesson inputs by schools officers include subjects such as crime and consequences, bullying, drugs, personal safety and offensive weapons. What school officers need to understand is how their inputs can form part of the National Curriculum for that school and complement the work of the teachers in teaching a consistent message – whether it be on drugs or bullying. In the past, many school officers have done this to great effect and as a result many schools became reliant upon their officer's contribution to the curriculum; however, this is now in jeopardy with the onset of school-based officers, due to other commitments being placed upon the school officer: patrols and truancy sweeps as well as dealing with incidents of antisocial behaviour in schools, previously dealt with by other officers or not reported in the first place. Many schools are reluctant to relinquish these 'teaching' officers and many officers are equally reluctant to change their roles from a purely educational role to that of a proactive police officer.

What is quite clear is that the provision of educational inputs as part of the officers role is an important one – but one that should not be the main source of their interaction with pupils.

There are a number of resources available to schools and police, which will assist in the development and delivery of citizenship; officers need to be aware of some of these materials and agencies.

One such example is the DfES website, which has schemes of work for schools on topics such as 'Young people and car crime'. This concentrates on investigating car crime and considers why young people become involved in crime and the consequences of their actions for their community as well as themselves. It also considers the role of the criminal justice system and the various agencies involved and allows the pupils to explore the work of 'expert witnesses', police officers, magistrates and court officials.

The Citizenship Foundation is also a good source of information for police officers offering advice around citizenship. They have published a 'Young Citizen's Passport', which contains a number of items that can be mapped to the National Curriculum for citizenship at Key Stage 4 and to the key skills qualifications. Examples of these learning activities can be viewed on the website *www.teachcitizenship.co.uk*

Other sites worth investigating include Rizer, which is a website being trialled in Nottinghamshire as a way in which police, youth workers and Connexions workers can work with young people. It offers information to offenders and those at risk of offending about the criminal justice system and focuses on areas such as crime and its consequences. The site is also very useful for citizenship lessons and is a good resource for all school officers. *www.rizer.co.uk*

A good example of this work has been undertaken in Camden, north London, where gifted and talented pupils from a local school took part in a two-day event on forensic science with the police and the forensic department of University College London. Pupils received talks from the police on criminal investigations and how to package evidence correctly; they also undertook a fingertip search of a crime scene near a mock grave, as well as learning about soil and vegetation analysis. Reports and witness statements were taken by the pupils; there were sessions on forensics science and how to present evidence, which resulted in a mock court session.

## Crimestoppers

Examples of other citizenship work available to officers include the work of Crimestoppers. The Crimestoppers Trust was formed in 1984 and is known to many through the visible advertising of its anonymous freefone telephone number 0800 555 111. The concept behind this number is that anyone is able to phone it and provide information about crime without having to give his or her details. The website *www.crimestoppers-uk.org/* provides fuller and up-to-date information of all topics discussed in this section.

What is probably less well known is that Crimestoppers do a great deal of work with young people. The Trust has a network of thirty-one regional volunteer groups in the UK, which work with young people to provide information and help raise the profile of Crimestoppers. This is delivered through projects in schools and in partnership with agencies as well as parents and young people themselves.

The projects run by the Trust for young people are designed to help reduce the level of youth crime and victimisation. The Trust has a number of specific aims:

- To provide targeted projects to different groups of young people to fulfil specific needs surrounding crime
- To increase young people's knowledge and understanding of Crimestoppers and to ensure the freefone 0800 555 111 number becomes 'information for life'
- To increase young people's responsibility to reduce and prevent crime in their communities, and to provide suggestions how to achieve this
- To understand the importance of giving information about criminal activity and that doing so is not an act of betrayal
- To educate young people about the implications of arrest and prosecution, and to show them how young people are dealt with by the criminal justice system
- To facilitate informed personal, moral and social choices.

Crimestoppers Trust, 2003

In addition, Crimestoppers Trust has developed a new citizenship-based educational resource called *Why should I?* It is aimed at Key Stage 3 and focuses on crime-related issues that affect young people as part of the citizenship curriculum and the resources available are free of charge.

*Why should I?* aims to provide choices to young people about situations that they may come across and how they should respond. It tackles issues such as graffiti, vandalism, teenage gangs and the cost of crime. There are also opportunities to explore the idea of social responsibility through drama, from an arts group that deliver an original piece of theatre to the pupils and then allows pupils an opportunity to interact with the actors. The Trust has also forged close links with the Youth Justice Board and encourages the use of this programme with young people attending

Youth Inclusion Programmes (YIPs) in order to raise awareness of Crimestoppers amongst the local community and enhance community safety.

These programmes are supported by the police as well as the current (2003) Minister for Education, Charles Clarke, who views it as an important way to forge good links between police and the community and, in particular, schools – in order to deal with issues such as truancy, exclusion and drug abuse. This is a free resource, which forms part of the National Curriculum in Citizenship, which school officers can promote in schools. Where appropriate, it can provide inputs to young people to help them understand how to respond appropriately to situations in which they may find themselves and to do the right thing for themselves and their community. There are a number of London schools, with a full-time schools officer, who have already adopted this programme.

For further information on this project contact:
*youthprojects@crimestoppers-uk.org*  telephone (020) 8254 3200.

Individual officers who form part of the SSP have also employed innovative methods to deal with problems arising in school, by incorporating citizenship as a theme for their work.

**CASE STUDY**

*In Barnet, North London, an SSP officer identified a group of pupils at the school who were at risk of exclusion and who had behaviour problems and displayed signs of becoming young offenders. The pupils attended a Pupil Referral Unit (PRU).*

*The officer wanted to identify a way of diverting the youths away from crime and to reduce their chances of exclusion whilst improving their attendance. With some assistance from Crime Concern, the officer selected six of the youths to participate in a street crime project, which resulted in as successful music video to be used in schools across London. It included the following lyrics:*

In these times
There's a lot of phone crimes
But jacking don't do nuthin though
They'll get the phone, get immobilised
The ultra-violet light will xpose u guys
Keep your phone in your pocket
Don't get victimised
Keep your eyes on those shy guys

Keep your things in ya pocket
Put a pin on it
Don't wanna get it thiefed then start to lock it
So you got a nice phone why u wana start to hot it
People on road got dey eye on it
Up against big gangs in street crime
Showing off ur phone giving off the wrong signs
When u get ur phone thiefed itz not nice
Don't show off ur phone, why pay da big price
So please start to think, think twice

Told you before and I'll tell you again
Don't go around thinking you're like them
Use your brain and don't try to be brave
Showing off things that others might crave.

*Lyrics written by six 13- to 14-years olds from the
Inclusion Unit at the Edgware School, Barnet*

**CASE STUDY**

*In Lambeth, south London, school police officers have made a
video with young people about mobile phone theft in response
to the NO CREDITS posters, which were put up around Lambeth
in the summer of 2002. To accompany the video there are a
series of lessons plans, which explore the main themes
portrayed, which include:*

- *Understanding the consequences of stealing and bullying*

- *Developing strategies to protect property*

- *To gain information about community service, tagging and
  mediation*

- *Gain confidence in dealing with bullies.*

## Youth Watch Scheme

In Somerset a school has become the first of its kind to host a school-
based Neighbourhood Watch Scheme in conjunction with its Crime
Reduction Police Officer.

The scheme embraces the subject of citizenship, by encouraging its
pupils to design posters and promote the scheme in order to deal with
problems that arise within the community. The scheme teaches pupils

how to become good citizens and encourages the use of Crimestoppers amongst pupils, should they become aware of crime incidents occurring in their school community. Sessions to date have included security-marking mobile phones and presentations on fire safety from the local fire department.

For more details contact PC Selby on 01823 363743 or visit the Ideas Exchange on the Crime Reduction Website at *www.crimereduction.gov.uk/iex*

Adapted from *Crime Reduction News,* July 2003

## Bullying conference

In Richmond upon Thames, London, school officers ran a conference for young people entitled *Bullying: Harmless fun or criminal act?* The aim of the project was to understand young people's perception of bullying and the law, to enable them to develop strategies to prevent and tackle bullying. The conference encompassed pupils from schools across the borough; it discussed their views and included theatre workshops and sessions on what was acceptable and unacceptable behaviour in the eyes of the law. The conference was held to be a success by the young people attending, who fed back their views through questionnaires and discussion groups. They stated that they now understood more about bullying and had developed some effective strategies for dealing with it, should they encounter such behaviour.

For further information contact Stuart Taylor, Metropolitan Police, London Borough of Richmond upon Thames. Email: Stuart.Taylor@met.police.uk

Taken from *Government Office for London Toolkit,* 2003

## Junior Citizenship

Since 1986, police services have been at the forefront of Junior Citizens, a multi-agency programme of activities designed to educate Year 6 pupils about a number of issues centred around safety. Some of the scenarios that the children encounter are 'stranger danger', where an adult approaches them and tries to lure them into his car -often with great ease. Others issues focus on the dangers of railways and safety in the home or near rivers and ponds. The pupils move from one scenario to another throughout the course of a day and, despite the cost and commitment needed to organise the event, Junior Citizenship is viewed by teachers, pupils and all agencies that participate as an extremely worthwhile activity.

In recent years, the cost of hosting such events has risen and sponsorship to finance the event appears to be even harder to come by. The police are beginning to devote even greater amounts of time to organising the two-week programme of activities, which are essentially multi-agency, and there are concerns that suitable accommodation is not always available to host such events.

The MPS are now looking to make the whole of Junior Citizenship more professional and to link it in with other activities for schools and the community as a whole. Through the offices of their Community Initiative Adviser they are looking to co-ordinate the setting up of a number of Community Education Centres in the MPS. The centres will be proactive, multi-agency and community-based delivering safety training; there will be a combination of a set of life-sized scenarios for safety training, with the addition of training facilities for activities such as First Aid courses and general health and safety training. The aim of the centres will be to make communities safer and they will cater for the needs of all sections of the community, although the main focus will be towards the Junior Citizenship programme.

Each centre's main feature would be an interactive street scene capable of delivering the following messages:

- Road safety
- Personal safety
- Safety in the home
- The consequences of crime on victims
- How vandalism and antisocial behaviour affect others
- Safety around railways
- Safety around water
- Danger on building sites
- Dangers of taking drugs and alcohol.

It is hoped that visitors to the centres would be exposed to some of the following messages:

- Taking responsibility
- Educating both adults and children to keep themselves safe
- Promotion of an understanding of others' needs
- Recognition of hazards, assessment of the risks and the taking steps to control those risks.

In addition to this, the sites will provide life skills and education, for a number of groups, including the elderly and disabled, to provide a response to the fear of crime and to minimise their vulnerability.

Other such sites already exist around the UK; they have proved to be extremely successful and give an indication of the work which can take place between partners to strengthen communities. School officers have a unique opportunity to make good use of such centres and provide professional guidance and support to the community, in particular Year 6 pupils, through the work of Junior Citizenship.

## Transition phase

One of the criticisms of the Safer School Partnership is the attention that some schools receive to the detriment of other schools. In particular, there is concern that some primary schools are not receiving as many visits from police officers – even though many of them form clusters for the SSP. A number of schools officers explain that, with the added workload they now encounter with a dedicated school, they are rarely able to visit primary schools. This does, however, differ between areas depending on the geographical location of primary schools to secondary schools and general workload.

Recently there has been some concern that Year 6 pupils, who are in their final year at primary school, have experienced a number of problems transferring to their respective secondary schools. It is a stage in many pupils' lives that causes them great concern and anxiety as they suddenly become the 'small fish in the big pool'. Some pupils have found this very hard to cope with and there have been a number of instances of pupils reacting to this change of environment by way of truancy, disruptive behaviour and disengagement with school life.

School officers can play an important part in ensuring that this transition phase is a smooth as possible by adopting a number of strategies. These include pencilling in a number of events at the secondary school which Year 6 pupils can attend, such as sports events, drama workshops and activity days. These all help the pupils familiarise themselves with the school setting and break down any fear and misconceptions that they may have. Although, of course, most schools already have general transition strategies in place, the SSP officer is able to concentrate on those pupils who the primary school have identified as being most at risk of becoming disengaged with school life.

In Hackney, north London, the SSP officers have introduced a unique scheme which targets a group of Year 6 pupils in one primary school who have been displaying a number of behavioural problems as identified by the school management team. This group of pupils attends a 'transition course' each Tuesday, for six weeks. The target group are each allowed to bring a class friend with them for company and encouragement; they participate in a number of outdoor activities such as kayaking and cycling at a nearby outward activity centre. Qualified staff supervise the morning activities, whilst the afternoon is devoted to classroom lessons run by the school-based officers. These lessons seek to address the pupils' behaviour and include sessions on crime and consequences, peer pressure, moral dilemmas and decision-making. The key to the programme is that the officers are the link between the pupils' primary and secondary schools. One of the faces that the pupils see on their first day at secondary school should be the familiar smile of their school officer.

## Extended school

Officers also have an opportunity to work with pupils as part of the extended school day. Many schools run breakfast clubs where they provide children with cereals and toast before school, to ensure that they have a proper meal before they start the school day. Officers can use this time to talk with pupils and get to know them better or help with the running of the club.

In other schools, particularly primary, the government has provided funding for schools to provide communities with a range of activities before, during and after school. This covers a whole range of services which school officers could participate in, and thus become a central part of the school community.

## Safer routes

The role of most school officers covers the period of time that pupils are at school, usually between 0800 and 1600 hours, Monday to Friday. Whilst the presence of officers in schools can have a positive effect on the amount of crime committed, there still exists the problem of protecting children outside of these hours – notably to and from school.

West Midlands Police have embarked upon a programme within a local private grammar school, situated in one of the most deprived areas of Birmingham. The pupils of this school had experienced a large number of robberies by local youths, who would attack them on their way to and from school. The use of traditional police methods to combat the problem had proved less than effective. An initiative was set up after consultation between the police and the school, entitled Safer Routes. The whole idea was to provide a safe route for pupils to walk between the local railway station, bus stops and the school, which police officers could patrol in the first instance to ensure the pupils' safety. Since the implementation of the scheme, there have been no robberies on the specified route despite the fact that the police now only patrol the route infrequently.

In Poole, Dorset, a number of schools have been working with the local school plans co-ordinator to look at safe and healthy ways to get to school; these include walking, bus escorts, school journey 'offers and requests' on a notice board by the school entrance, car sharing, and a 'bicycle train'.

In the Isle of Wight, they have come up with a novel idea of dealing with young people who act in a 'threatening, abusive or disruptive manner' aboard regular school buses. The punishment they face is to be forced to travel to school on a 'pink' bus and in addition the buses heating may be removed and journeys extended by five minutes for every offence that the driver happens to notice. (Owen, G 2003). The concept behind this is quite simply that pupils will feel ashamed to be driven to and from school on a pink bus and this will change their behaviour accordingly.

In an age where image is everything, this may just be effective. It echoes the voices of many children who complain about being driven around in school and council buses, which they associate with disadvantaged and elderly groups and deem to be 'uncool' or 'lame'. On occasions where truancy sweeps were conducted in London with police officers and educational welfare officers, pupils would make themselves known to the truancy team when they saw them driving around parks and open spaces in smart new Mercedes buses equipped with CD players and quadraphonic speakers. The reverse was true when they saw yellow council buses with the local authority's name down the side.

The extent to which one should expose children to such ridicule is debatable. It remains to be seen whether, over time, such treatment would lose its effectiveness and to travel on 'the bus' would become almost a status symbol. As one observer noted 'This is the modern equivalent of putting them in the stocks.'

On a more positive note, officers in the London borough of Hackney have initiated a project which aims to reduce the level of victimisation, in particular street robbery and bullying for young people on their way to and from school. The project, targeted in secondary schools in the borough, also aims to reduce the fear of crime for these young people; it is conducted by school officers within the Safer School Partnership. These officers plan safer routes for the pupils and highlight areas of concern such as abandoned cars, poor lighting and changes in regular police patrols in order to prevent and reduce crime on these routes. In addition, school officers patrol the school community before and after school and enjoy the assistance of the police community support officers.

> Other information on safer routes can be obtained from the following organisations:
>
> - SUSTRANS, the national charity, set up to promote Safe Routes to School, and walking and cycling initiatives. Telephone (0117) 915 0100
> - The Young TransNet website provides an opportunity for young people to explore transport issues. *www.youngtransnet.org.uk* or telephone (020) 7843 6325
> - The Pedestrians' Association also gives excellent advice on walking routes to school. Contact them at 31-33 Bondway, London SW8 1SJ.

## The SAFEMark Awards

This is a South Yorkshire Initiative, which stands for Supporting A Friendly Environment.

The award is granted to those schools that demonstrate concern about, and implement a structured response to, their particular school transport issues.

The programme revolves around key agencies working together to demonstrate good practice in home-to-school transport for pupils. The partnership includes a number of key agencies that come together to ensure that the scheme operates and include the police, support staff, schools, and bus operators. There are several stages for the partnership to work through with the school, which include:

- Getting organised
- How the school manages the issues
- Working with pupils

- Using the curriculum
- Involving the community
- Applying the law.

The school receive inputs from trained consultants as part of PSHE lessons, which include how to behave on buses, dealing with issues of bullying and crime and their effect of their behaviour on other people and respect for others.

The police, along with identified teachers and wardens, patrol the bus stops and shelters to ensure that pupils are waiting in an orderly manner and conducting themselves properly while the bus operators give an undertaking that they will send out, and on time, the correct buses, and that the drivers will report incidents to police if they occur.

There are two pilot projects about to take place in London with an expectation that such a programme can be offered to all schools in the capital.

## Prison visits

A popular method of educating pupils about the dangers of a life of crime appears to be prison visits or, conversely, prisoners visiting schools. Pentonville Prison in Islington, London, regularly allows prisoners accompanied by prison guards to visit schools and give well-rehearsed presentations which focus on the harsh reality of prison life. Serving inmates bring examples of food rations and everyday items such as razors and phone cards, which they regard as luxuries. A canvas mat is laid on the classroom floor measuring approximately eight foot by six foot; this has the prisoner's bed, sink and toilet marked out on it. The cells house two men and pupils are invited to walk across the mat with another classmate without bumping into them and trying to avoid the furniture.

This insight into the reality and harshness of prison life is a real eye-opener for the pupils who come face-to-face with issues of lack of privacy, prison-issued clothing, food rationing, isolation and a loss of liberty.

A reporter from the *Times Educational Supplement* followed a group of young offenders around HMP Coldingly for the day, in an attempt to see at first hand what the prisoners incarcerated in a world of their own can teach young people who are at risk from falling into a life of crime. The message seems to be 'prison is not the place for you'. (*TES*, July 2000).

The presentation consists of dramas, songs and personal testimonies and its organisers boldly claim that it's 'the best crime diversion scheme in the country'. The prisoners appear to benefit from their presentations and many of them are using the pilot scheme to work towards accreditation for basic youth work skills.

One of the inmates explains 'Someone could have got to me when I was their age, with a different approach. All we had in South London was the local bobby'. The inmates are graphic in their description of the harsh reality of prison life 'It's fucking shit in here, man, and YOIs (Young Offender Institutes) are worse. Every one of us wishes we were your age again. We're not here to fucking patronise any of you. All we're saying to you is that you've got choices.' (*TES*, July 2000).

However, research suggests that programmes of brief encounters with inmates describing the brutality of prison life or short-term incarceration in prisons or jails, which are intended to shock, do not work. Studies which observed the work of Scared Straight, a youth violence prevention strategy widely used in the USA revealed that the programme does not deter future criminal activities and that re-arrest rates were similar between controls and youths who participated in the same Scared Straight. In others, youths exposed to Scared Straight actually had higher rates of re-arrest than youths not involved in this intervention. (Surgeon General, 2001)

There is conflicting evidence about the value of presentations to children by serving prisoners to 'Scare straight or educate', as examined in a research document by the Home Office 1996. The research focused on three case studies at three prisons, with presentations tending to focus on the 'depressing and brutal nature of prison life.'

One of the key points is that, although there appears to be no hard evidence that similar projects in the US have had any real impact on the reoffending of juveniles, there does appear to be considerable potential for developing day-visit projects that aim to educate rather than scare.

## Alternative curriculum

I refer in particular to my own work with a group of pupils at a secondary school in a London borough, which was the subject of a BBC documentary entitled *Classrooms at War*. This programme outlined my work with a small group of Year 10 pupils over a period of two school terms and showed how participation in the scheme had helped the pupils with their behaviour, participation and attendance in school. Other work, which I conducted with pupils who had either been in trouble with the authorities or who had difficulty socialising in school, was equally successful in enabling pupils to address their associated behaviours. A review of this was outlined in the *Times Educational Supplement*, 31 March 2000.

Similar attempts to engage pupils in an alternative curriculum vary greatly in their style, delivery and potential successes. Two further examples of such schemes designed for disaffected children or those who are perceived to be at risk are described here.

> There is a scheme run by several army officers, who work with the pupils towards basic key skills which are incorporated into the bronze and silver Award Scheme Development and Accreditation Networks (ASDAN) syllabus, together with the Bronze Duke of Edinburgh's award, the St John's lifesaver awards and some outdoor environmental experience. After six months on the scheme, it is reported that the participants' behaviour 'has improved beyond all recognition'. Additional benefits have seen marked improvements in the pupils' GCSE curricular work.
>
> *The Guardian Education*, 13 March 2001

> Police officers in Durham run a scheme which engages 'young tearaways' in the art of fishing. It aims to 'influence attitudes and try to persuade youngsters to move from negative peer groups into positive groups.' The scheme is supported by senior police management, who are trying to provide the youngsters with a scheme which is not just run on an occasional basis but is something more substantial and beneficial to the youngsters. 'Angling can give a lad a chance. I know from my own experience that it helps. Youngsters from a bad peer group meet lads of their own age behaving in a positive way. That's good for them, it's good for the sport and society has to benefit'.
>
> Clarke, 2000

There are, of course, time constraints imposed upon such activities and thorough risk assessments are needed; however, despite the numerous roles that the school officer now undertakes, there is always the opportunity to assist with such schemes – both in school holidays as well as part of a structured curriculum during term time. This is particularly attractive to those officers who have outward bound skills and who are used to organising team-building days and problem-solving activities to boost esteem and encourage young people to participate and try something new and challenging. The schemes are a good source of diversion for pupils who simply cannot engage in school life and who tend to display signs of disruption when at school.

## Drugs

The MPS 'Drug Strategy 2003-2006' has two main strands: reducing supply and reducing demand. In order to reduce demand the MPS aims to ensure that we make an effective contribution, where appropriate, to drug awareness education and prevention programmes. This new policy is designed to deliver a consistent drug education programme, MPS-wide. This policy is of particular relevance to school officers, who will have specific responsibilities for ensuring that the policy is complied with. They will be the main source of delivering drugs education in schools and therefore it is essential that they are delivering an accurate and *consistent* message.

Recent research into school drug education (O'Connor L, et al, 2001) identified the fact that police officers are not the *prime* deliverers of drug education in schools and also that they should not be delivering any moral or health aspects of drugs education. Their core expertise falls, as might be expected, within laws and procedures (legal status, classes of drugs, stop and search), criminal consequences (case disposal options and significance, penalties attached to convictions and local trends including association between drugs and crime), and drugs recognition (showing images and placebo samples, ensuring that its context is set within the first two areas). By adopting this policy, school officers will deliver a consistent message about drugs to children, and help raise awareness for teachers and school governors. This, in turn, should lead to improved partnerships and clearer roles for police officers around drugs education.

It is, therefore, important that schools officers work in close partnership with other agencies when planning and delivering drugs education. This can be achieved by liasing with the PSHE co-ordinator or being present when other agencies deliver lessons. It would be desirable for schools officers to actually meet up with these agencies at the beginning of term, to ensure that they are aware of each other's work and that no duplication takes place or, more importantly, that no contradictory messages are given out to pupils. This will reinforce the officers' key responsibilities and avoid them straying into areas outside their expertise, where they might have, in the past, been used to fill the 'learning gap'.

## Drugs dogs

There are currently two police forces using passive drugs detection dogs on a regular basis in schools in Kent and Thames Valley. This is in response to requests from head teachers, who are becoming increasingly concerned over the number of drug-related incidents in schools.

In other forces, passive dogs are used only for pre-planned operations to detect drugs in public places such as railway stations and outside pubs and clubs. However, there appear to be a growing number of requests for the deployment of these dogs within the school setting, which raises a number of issues. In response to this, the MPS have set out a guideline for schools wishing to use passive drugs dogs. School officers need to be aware of this and should insist that their forces have such guidelines in place to deal with the use of passive drugs dogs.

It might be thought that simply having a police officer on site would detract from the smoking or possession of cannabis within the confines of the school; from experience, however, this is not the case and pupils will still smoke it in the toilets before and during school, which causes a number of discipline problems.

On many occasions it is the head teacher of a school who approaches the police to enquire whether a drugs dog can be used in the school to help deal with the problem of drug-taking. If this is the case then it would be remiss of police authorities not to respond to this request to help resolve a problem. Forces need to have a protocol in place (which forms part of their Drug Education Policy) that they can share with the school, which addresses the deployment of such a resource. According to the MPS Drugs Strategy, the protocol should include a risk assessment that covers, amongst other things:

- School's legal position
- Preservation of educational rights and inclusive practice
- Parental permission
- Searches of young people, staff and property
- Media involvement
- Support services and pastoral care
- Health and safety

- Disclosure, confidentiality and rights to privacy
- Monitoring and evaluation process.

More information on drugs-related issues can be obtained from:

**Childline**
telephone: 0800 1111
*www.childline.org.uk*

**National Drugs Helpline**
telephone: 0800 77 66 00
*www.ndh.org.uk*

**Bullying Online**
*www.bullying.co.uk*

## Safer surfing

There have been a number of recent reports in the media about the dangers of the Internet, in particular to those children who regularly use chat rooms to talk to other people on their home computers. A recent case highlights the growing concern that often children do not know who they are actually talking to: a young girl flew from England to Paris, to meet up with an American ex-marine, twice her age, with whom who she had 'chatted' and exchanged details over the Internet. Children often give out private information about themselves and their movements to other Internet users; although in the majority of cases this is between other children of a similar age, there are instances where adults and paedophiles have posed as children in an attempt to befriend children and 'groom' them for sex. Note that, mid-2003, draft legislation is in place to make grooming a criminal offence under the Sexual Offences Bill.

There have been numerous campaigns in the daily newspapers, as well as advertisements on national television, attempting to educate children – and their parents – about the safe use of the Internet. However, with a high percentage of children having access to the Internet, often unsupervised and within the confines of their own rooms, concerns are still being raised.

In the London borough of Ealing, schools officers have developed a unique package to help educate children, teachers and parents about the safe use of the Internet, which involves participating in a classroom lesson with pupils on the subject of chat rooms. The officer logs onto a chat room via his portable laptop and allows pupils to communicate, under a pseudonym, with another teenager in the chat room. The lesson is led by the class, who decide what to write in response to the other person in the chat room. At the conclusion of the lesson the pupils are confronted by this unknown person – who is, in fact, another police officer in an adjoining room, linked into their website. What this officer then reveals is how easy it has been to extract information from the pupils in relation to their name, age, sex, location, phone number and address, whilst posing as a teenager himself. Pupils often claim that they had given the mystery person false information about themselves, but this only serves to reinforce the point that if they are prepared to lie with the assumption that they will be believed, then so is someone who has more sinister motives.

The sudden appearance of the police officer from an adjoining room serves as a real shock to many of the pupils, who are surprised at the ease with which someone can pose as a child and extract information. Although shock tactics are not necessarily the best way in which to prevent or educate children about inherent dangers, the pupils in this example do appear to sit up and listen and take note of the next part of the lesson, which concentrates on informing pupils how to surf the net safely.

A similar package is being created for parents to help make them familiar with computers and the Internet: there is concern that many parents do not know how to operate computers and have little understanding of the Internet or how to supervise their children whilst using it.

## Gun crime

It cannot go without notice that there has been a significant rise in the number of serious crimes involving the use of guns. There has also been a noticeable rise in the number of young people carrying replica and imitation handguns in the street and within the school community. These are often fashion accessories, used to impress their peers, but on an increasing number of occasions these 'toys' are being used in robberies and are fast becoming a status symbol associated with a gangster lifestyle.

The present government is deeply concerned and has devised a London-wide anti-crime initiative, with a view to promoting an anti-gun message through its gun crime reduction strategy, by engaging with young people. It is also introducing new legislation to combat the carrying of replica guns and air weapons.

The Greater London Authority is developing an initiative to target individuals and communities that would be very effective in tackling the culture of gun crime amongst young people. It has created an education package for use in schools and youth clubs which includes music CDs, video clips, lesson plans, researched articles and a website. It is intended to roll the package out to schools through trained volunteers.

Although schools officers will not necessarily receive extensive training in this area, it is still important that they have an understanding of the fundamental issue underlying gun culture and ways in which to approach the subject with young people

The West Midlands police force is currently tackling this issue by forging links with schools, clubs and community centres in an effort to focus on young people and gun crime as part of the government's well-publicised gun amnesties.

## Independent advisory groups

Many police forces are now introducing the concept of Independent Advisory Groups, which are set up to canvas the views of the general public about issues in general that relate to policing the particular area. In the Metropolitan Police, Lambeth Borough Youth Council are helping to create a force-wide advisory group of young people. A one-day workshop held at New Scotland Yard was attended by over a hundred 14 to 18-year olds, accompanied by their school beat officers; they participated in workshops, discussions and syndicate groups.

This is an invaluable way of communicating with young people and canvassing their ideas and feelings on a whole range of subjects and issues. School beat officers are invariably the key, along with the teacher, to ensuring that young people are able to attend such meetings and have their thoughts and feelings heard by people in a position of authority – people who have the opportunity to shape policy. It is, therefore, imperative that school beat officers take the opportunity of participating in such events and they should actively encourage young people to attend. It is a great opportunity to hear their thoughts and to understand what lies behind many of the issues that affect this section of the population – which the police, along with other parts of the community, are often unable to engage with.

## Joint training

There are many training opportunities open to teachers, education staff and police officers, as opposed to education for schoolchildren; some of the more usual topics are listed here.

### Restorative justice

A large number of Safer Schools officers have now been trained up in the use of restorative practices in schools, which usually take the form of a 'conference' with the affected parties. One of the initial pilots for restorative justice was used in a school in Banbury, Oxfordshire with a catchment area of a local estate where there were incidents of violence, combined with huge social deprivation. Despite these problems there had been some excellent relations built up between the school and the local police, who together had managed to tackle bad behaviour amongst its pupils.

The police first suggested the concept of restorative justice to deal with pupils misbehaving and, before too long, the school started to see real results. The head teacher outlines two such examples. A child racially abused a member of staff and had to apologise in front of his mother. 'In the past, that would have meant an automatic exclusion. But we used restorative justice and it worked brilliantly. The pupil has not been in trouble since,' remarked the head. In another incident, a young girl assaulted another pupil at school; after a restorative justice conference she was engaged in helping to improve the security of the school. (Brown M, 2002)

There are now emerging many similar examples of officers undertaking effective restorative justice conferences across the country, but there does not appear to be a system in place for collating these meetings and recording their outcomes. It would be useful to know how much of the officers' time is spent organising these conferences, how many they undertake and whether or not there is any follow up to see whether the child has re-offended, or come to the notice of the school, since the event. Initial apologies and remorse is a stepping-stone but, in terms of the money, time and resources spent on restorative justice conferences, officers need to ensure that they are effective in the long term.

This could be best achieved by effective monitoring of the conferences: a form should be completed outlining the nature of the conference, the dates and identification of those who participated (along with contact numbers) and the outcomes or agreements arrived. These can be followed up six months later to investigate whether the child has come to notice; the effect of the restorative justice conference, in terms of improving their behaviour or offending, can thus be more objectively ascertained.

```
SAMPLE FORM

Name of pupil _____

Name of teacher _____

Name of police officer _____

Name of parent _____


Contact details _____

School _____

Year _____

Offence _____

Outcome _____

Agreement _____

General comments _____

Time allocated to planning and delivering conference _____
```

Similar work around restorative justice has been used in primary schools to deal with bad behaviour and other related problems that are experienced in schools. In primary schools in Oxfordshire, police have introduced the concept of a 'healing circle'. This was used to great effect after a series of thefts in class: the officer encouraged the pupils, in turn, to share with the others what had been stolen and how they felt about it. The class had to offer solutions to the problem, but all of the proceedings revolve around the pupils speaking only when they are in possession of the 'healing stone'.

According to the head teacher, these healing sessions reflect traditional circle times and provide the 'seed bed' for the skills to allow a system of restorative justice to work. (Brown M, 2002)

More information on this topic can be obtained from:

*www.transformingconflict.org*
*www.teachernet.gov.uk/pshe*
*www.dfes.gov.uk/citizenship*

## Critical incidents

There have been a number of incidents occurring in schools where officers have had to think about preserving crime scenes – not always an easy job in a thriving and vibrant school of over a thousand children. Crime scenes have, all too often, been disturbed by well-meaning caretakers who have endeavoured to return the school to normality by washing away any evidence under a mop of water or removing broken glass to prevent any injuries to children.

In Westminster, school officers have taken the opportunity to make a presentation for school staff all about preserving crime scenes; they have placed a critical incident bag within the school to assist in the event of such an incident, containing essential items such as gloves, tape and basic first aid. What was noticeable from speaking to the officer was how much the staff enjoyed learning about such areas of police work; one of the major benefits from the training was the good relationships that were forged as a result of it.

Whilst considering critical incidents there is also a need for school officers to consider the forensics opportunities that may be applicable at a school incident. Officers in Ealing, west London, have made good use of a digital camera to capture the work of vandals and graffiti sprayed on walls and fences. On a number of occasions these have been stored and linked up with other incidents around the borough, revealing the same 'tag' – the distinctive signature or embellishment used to sign each piece of graffiti. Other forensic opportunities are explored later in the section on arson.

## Child protection

All school staff receive child protection training at school, but there should always be a designated teacher who deals with all child protection issues at the school. In Haringey, London, an officer trained in child protection helped to train up a number of newly qualified teachers at the school on the actions to consider taking in the event of a child protection issue arising. This led to requests to provide more training, specifically around the issues of identifying children at risk, supporting vulnerable witnesses and supporting victims of crime. Since the inception of the SSP, many teachers and officers have called for a greater understanding of how to deal with children who are suffering from mental illnesses or those who are merely disruptive or temperamental in class. Numerous studies have been written about the factors which affect young people and influence their daily lives, and it is essential that police and teachers have a far greater understanding of what makes young people 'tick', if we are to assist them

outcomes for children who suffer from mental illnesses. If such problems are not identified, then this can lead to school or home breakdown, as well as emotional and conduct problems emerging from unrecognised learning difficulties.

According to a DfES document, *Promoting Children's Mental Health within Early Years and School Settings* (2003),

> 'There is often a poor long-term outcome for children who have disruptive behaviour problems if their difficulties go untreated, with a greater likelihood of these children becoming involved in crime, alcohol and drug-related problems and having severe relationship difficulties in adulthood'.

It is therefore important for school officers to understand some of the main issues that underline mental health. These include:

- What is mental health?
- Mental health difficulties
- Risk factors in the child, family and community
- Resilience factors
- Key characteristics for schools that promote young people's mental health
- Dealing with individual student needs
- Special educational needs – code of practice
- Support for schools
- Specialist mental health professionals.

This is a complex area – one with which school officers need to become familiar, and one which needs to be developed into a training package, so that officers are able to identify key risk and resilience factors for young people are suffering from mental health issues and provide them with the necessary support through appropriate professionals. The link between crime and children who suffer from mental health is one which officers need to understand; a failure to act or identify such conditions will result in more children becoming involved in crime and reducing their chances of a successful life and career.

In addition to these topics, the training most frequently requested within schools which benefit from a SRO includes:

- The role of School Beat Officers
- Reducing crime through a problem-solving approach
- Acceptable behaviour contracts/parental control agreements
- Drug awareness
- Safer surfing
- Achieving best evidence (ABE)
- Behaviour management
- Risk assessment
- Crimestoppers
- Arson in schools
- Understanding work with young people and the role of Connexions
- Domestic violence and its effects on children
- Bullying and homophobia.

## Adviser

### Faith groups

This is not an area that one would naturally associate with police work; its relevance to a school's work would seem even further detached. Interest in this area first came to public attention in Haringey, north London, through the work of the local pastors who formed the Haringey Peace Alliance in response to the growing number of gun-related incidents. According to Metropolitan Police statistics, five people had been shot dead and gun crime had risen by 12% during the period 2002-2003.

The work of the alliance was to pray for their community and address issues in the borough, particularly in relation to young people. So effective were the prayers for the local people, which culminated in a 'Peace Week', that the local police reported a reduction of 47% of violent crime involving firearms thanks to the combined work of the police and churches in the area. The then borough commander of Haringey police highlighted the power of prayer as an important factor in achieving this result; in a recent breakfast launch entitled *Active faith: Safer communities,* the Deputy Commissioner of the Metropolitan Police, Sir Ian Blair, echoed the need for prayer in our communities. He promoted the 'Hope for London' initiative, which concentrates on what can happen when 'Christians pray for their neighbours and communities and act on those prayers, to address the challenge of crime in their part of the city.'

## Making a PACT

In Nottinghamshire, Police and Churches Together (PACT) formed an alliance in 2001 which saw a 40% drop in juvenile crime over a two-year period. This was achieved, according to the local police inspector, through prayer and commitment from the community. 'I put prayer at the top of the reasons for change, along with very hard work by the local police, combined with the local community'.

A similar initiative took place in 1997, also in Nottinghamshire, where again youth-related crime in one local area appeared to drop on a Wednesday night. It transpired that one of the local churches was giving out free pizza to children who happened to be hanging out by the church with little else to do. Other churches were encouraged to join in the scheme and, combined with prayer, there was a 10% drop in crime overall in the area – juvenile crime in particular.

## Adopt a Cop

This scheme links police officers with their churches through prayer. The churches adopt an officer and pray for the officer's personal and policing needs. This is something that many officers may find strange or difficult to accept as part of their working practice. Fiona Mactaggart, MP, shared such cynicism when she delivered a speech at the 2003 launch of 'Active Faith – Safer Communities'. However, midway through her speech she revealed that she did not believe in a 'God', but that she was constantly reminded by members of her constituency that they were praying for her, particularly in relation to the treatment that she was undergoing for cancer. She then revealed that she had visited her doctor that week and had been told that she was in full remission. She explained that this turn of events had certainly made her think about the power of prayer... She was thanked by the Chair for her testimony, albeit unintentional.

## Clapham

In Clapham, London, the local Methodist Church opened its doors to children in the area for an after-school club which provided a safe environment to play, learn and do homework. The church feel strongly that children need after-school activities to keep them busy and stimulated in order to avoid boredom and the risk of drifting into trouble. At present it is attempting to expand its project work and open up a breakfast club, which would ensure youngsters get something to eat first thing in the morning to help them last the day at school – and encourage them to come to school in the first place.

## N'flame

These are all key areas that schools officers can become engaged in; although the activities listed are Christian-based, there are a number of other faith groups that are opening their doors to the wider community in order to reduce crime. It is in areas like these that schools officers can have a significant impact through their links with schools and the local community. They are perfectly positioned to make these links with young people and the churches, and to bring the two together for the benefit of all. There is plenty of help at hand for officers wishing to develop these links through charities and agencies such as N'flame who are a Christian-based organisation that operate in north London. The team members work in secondary schools, with the aim of providing the pupils with a positive experience of Christian role models. They provide 'roots clubs' which is a lunchtime club for Christian students to meet and have fellowship with each other, as well as providing inputs in assemblies about Christianity and the Church, and offering an insight as to who Christ is. Lessons provide the opportunity to explore these themes further and see how they relate to modern-day issues of abortion and the environment. They also run a series of bullying workshops, very popular with schools, which involve drama and help pupils explore the issues of bullying and how it affects them. In March 2003 they set up a prayer diary for schools in Enfield when they met outside a number of the secondary schools and prayed for each school individually and its specific needs.

Several school beat officers have worked in partnership with N'flame to develop these activities in their school and have found this to be very rewarding. The bullying workshops have been an excellent way of addressing an area which causes many children a great deal of anguish, and which is often the start of more sinister intimidation – and the causes of some pupils not fully engaging in school and potentially truanting. Their style of delivery is a much more effective way of educating pupils than the police officers can ever hope to achieve and the reception that the team receive is testament to their teaching skills and knowledge of the subject matter.

This is not a one-off thing for church-based organisations to be engaged with; in fact, there are numerous bodies that are providing activities for teenagers across the country. School beat officers need to be aware of the organisations that can assist with engaging young people and to which they can refer them: examples include Crusaders, Youth for Christ and the Oasis Trust, which run outdoor activities and summer camps, as well as working in schools to help prevent social exclusion and enabling children to access sports, the arts – or simply have an area in which to hang out. (Gregory H, 2003).

For more information on some of these topics, look at:

**Haringey Peace Alliance**
telephone: (020) 8808 9439
*www.peacealliance.org.uk*

**PACT** (Police and Churches Together) in Newark, Nottingham
telephone: (0115) 967 0555 ex 7660
*Jeremy.Butler@nottinghamshire.pnn.police.uk*

**Adopt a Cop** Christian Police Association (CPA), London
Inspector Bob Pull
telephone: (020) 7230 6150
*cpa@met.police.uk  www.cpmet.org.uk*

**N'flame**
telephone: (020) 8886 7859
*n.flame@talk21.com  www.nflame.org.uk*

**Oasis Trust**
telephone: (020) 7450 9000
*www.oasistrust.org*

**Evangelical Alliance**
telephone: (020) 7207 2100
*www.eauk.org*

**Crusaders**
telephone: (01582) 589850
*www.crusaders.org.uk*

**Youth For Christ**
telephone: (0121) 550 8055
*www.yfc.co.uk*

## Problem solving

Problem solving is a way of improving situations by degrees, which is referred to as the *Impact Scale*. This scale means:

- Eliminating a problem *or*
- Reducing a problem by x%; *or*
- Reducing the seriousness of a problem; *or*
- Dealing with a problem more efficiently; *or*
- Persuading another organisation to take the lead.

Problem solving in police work has been around for at least twenty years and has been successfully used all over the world. It works by identifying and dealing with the root causes of a problem instead of repeatedly responding to the consequences. Police and partners, working together, can use problem solving to manage crime, reduce the number of calls police have to deal with, reduce collisions and improve the general quality of life (e.g. by getting rid of abandoned cars, vandalism, graffiti etc.).

The Metropolitan Police Service, who now lead the way in problem solving, have drawn upon best practice around the world to design a simple but effective Problem Solving Process (PSP) for school officers to use. There is also a PSP file (shown in the appendix as Form 302) that one can use to record the process. This form is available for both police and their partners.

At present, school officers are being trained alongside teachers and partners from Youth Offending Teams (YOTs) and agencies such as Connexions in order to find solutions to problems in the school community; these may include vandalism at bus stops, antisocial behaviour and graffiti. The PSP is an excellent way in which to capture the work which agencies undertake when problem solving. The final product can serve as an example of best practice that can be shared with other schools officers and agencies when it comes to tackling similar problems across the country.

For more information on problem solving contact:

**MPS Problem Solving Unit**
Territorial Policing Headquarters
Victoria Embankment
London SW1 2JL
telephone: 020 7321 9033
*problemsolvingunit@met.police.uk*

## School safety: emergency planning

School officers need to ensure that their schools are safe and secure at all times from risk of attack from those intent on committing crimes such as vandalism, assault, arson and burglary. Crime prevention is the key to success and in this respect school officers should link in closely with their Crime Prevention Officer who can advise them how to secure a school and will undertake a full school safety survey in partnership with the school.

The survey is very comprehensive and will make a list of

recommendations that will cover areas such as exterior lighting, CCTV, doors and locks, car parking arrangements, natural surveillance including fences, and property marking schemes.

In addition to this, the school officer can conduct surveys with the staff and pupils around areas of the school which need to be looked at because they are hidden or insecure and attract trespassers, or antisocial or criminal behaviour.

The officer also needs to work in partnership with the school management team to ensure that they are aware of emergency evacuation drills and what to do if there is a fire or other emergency on the school site. This could include instances where schools come under attack from gangs of youths from other schools or simply from irate parents or pupils who become out of control and a danger to themselves and other members of the school community. In today's climate one cannot rule out suspect packages, bomb threats or stalkers within the school trying to befriend young victims and lure them away. And one must never forget that both the Dunblane and Hungerford massacres took place, in part at least, on school premises.

It is therefore proposed that school officers should work with the schools to produce school plans, which can be stored in the control room at the police station and allow officers attending the school to access all parts of it as quickly as possible. This is especially true of large or multi-site locations, where, for example, the art studio or chemistry lab may not be at all obvious from a main entrance. As previously mentioned in this book it is also a good idea for officers to encourage their sector colleagues to come into the school on a regular basis so that they not only get to know the layout of the school, but also become a familiar face with the staff and pupils and help break down barriers between the police and young people.

## Partnership links

### Fire Brigade

A guide, *How to combat arson in schools* has been published on the home office crime reduction website *http://www.crimereduction.gov.uk/arson10.htm* but is also of relevance to the school beat officer. Below are a few of the facts surrounding arsons at schools and some practical advice that officers can give to schools and their partners and tools for development.

There is a five-point action plan for preventing arson attacks:

- Deter unauthorised entry onto the site
- Prevent unauthorised entry into the building
- Reduce the opportunity for the offender to start a fire
- Reduce the scope for potential fire damage
- Reduce subsequent losses and disruption resulting from a fire.

These points are now discussed in greater detail.

### Deter unauthorised entry onto the site

This can be achieved by liasing with the crime prevention officer, who can assist with offering advice about the use of signs and clearly marked boundaries around the school, accompanied with signs, so that trespassers are aware of their actions. In addition, advice on lighting and security cameras can be offered and suggestions regarding patrols of the school by the officer and caretaker, especially after the hours of darkness.

### Prevent unauthorised entry into the building

Initially this depends on the design of the school; where situations arise that buildings have a number of vulnerable spots, such as recesses or alcoves, and then additional lighting may need to be considered. Good security locks – on doors as well as windows and their frames and roof lights – should be installed. The presence of alarms are also a great deterrent – but only when they are responded to. Encourage neighbours who make it their duty to keep an 'eye out' for the school or the Neighbourhood Watch or School Watch schemes. CCTV is another piece of technology that can be very effective, but only if they work or cover the areas that are most vulnerable and likely to attack. Where relevant, check tapes regularly to ensure that recordings are actually being made and that they are of sufficiently high quality to have evidential value. Ensure that tapes are archived, off site, for a sufficiently long period.

### Reduce the opportunity for the offender to start a fire

This includes ensuring that refuse containers are locked and secure and positioned far enough away for the school not to be a danger if ignited. The same is true for any other material which may be combustible, as well as sheds or liquid stores such as heating oil or petroleum.

### Reduce the scope of potential fire damage

If a fire starts, it is important to be able to minimise the potential effect that the fire may have by containing it to a specified area. Much of this will depend on the design of the school although the school officer can assist by seeing that expensive equipment is put away safely in a secure separate room, which may be better guarded from the risks of fire.

### Reduce subsequent losses

This entails ensuring that the correct equipment is available and that members of staff are suitably trained in fire procedures and know how to summon the fire brigade, evacuate buildings and use fire extinguishers. Staff should also know where the high-value materials are stored, including records that may be irreplaceable, and be aware of a salvage plan to recover the items. In the event of a fire, a service recovery plan would be needed and should include:

- Details of people who can help in an emergency
- Information of suppliers
- Inventory of equipment
- How media enquiries can be handled.

School officers have a responsibility to work in partnership with the Fire Brigade to reduce the number of fires caused in schools  According to a Home Office survey conducted by the Arson Prevention Bureau in 1995, nearly 75% of school fires were the result of malicious fires with 45% of these occurring in secondary schools, despite them only representing 15% of all schools. 10% of schools are subject to more than one attack (usually secondary schools) and although 61% of fires occurred outside the normal school day of 8am to 4pm, a high number still occurred in secondary schools in the afternoon between 1pm and 3pm. It is also worthy of note that, in 84% of the cases of school fires, many schools had reported incidents of criminal damage, theft and burglary in the twelve months leading up to the fire. The involvement of school officers in this process is self-evident and partnerships need to be established with the Fire Brigade if they are to help in some way with the subject of arson in schools.

### Support staff

School officers need to learn to rely on others to help them undertake their role in the school community. Such help can come from a number of sources which reflect the partnership approach to making school communities safer. One school officer based in a school in west London has begun to work in partnership with a colleague in the Metropolitan Special Constabulary. Traditionally, Specials tend to work at evenings and weekends, as many of them have careers outside of the police service; some assist on busy Friday and Saturday nights, at football matches or other commitments and are a much-valued source of assistance to the regular officers. However, one Special has been working with a schools officer, helping him at the end of the school day with any problems that occur both inside and outside the school. Flash points were usually opposite the school in the park or directly outside the school gates. Together, the officers are able to provide a greater show of strength and ultimately deal more effectively with incidents that arise. Examples of these have been dispersing large crowds of pupils, breaking up minor scuffles and subduing incidents of public order.

It is essential for the officer that both the schools and the general public see that the school officer is not working in isolation. This is particularly relevant in terms of safety for the officer as well as providing him with a good support network. The role of the school officer is very similar to that of officers seconded to the Youth Offender Team, in that they are usually the only police officers working within that environment and this can cause a wide-ranging number of problems: police officers are suddenly immersed in a culture which is not their own and often they do not know how to react and have very little understanding of how to operate. They become subject to different regulations and working practices (as well as their own). Through time, this becomes not only confusing but also extremely difficult to retain one's identity as a police officer.

The presence of other police personnel not only provides companionship, but also reinforces the officer's identity and authority and enables them to collectively fulfil their roles. In terms of safety, it also provides the school officer with a 'back up' and another pair of eyes and sends out the message that the officer has other people who support and will assist whenever the need arises.

Officers in Hackney have called upon the services of the Police Community Safety Officers to work alongside them, in a bid to undertake their role more effectively. They assist the school officers with their patrols and are a visible presence and a source of contact for the school community.

## Wardens

Wardens can also play an important part in assisting school officers, especially in dealing with incidents around the school at bus stops and when dealing with antisocial behaviour. In Haringey, they are used extensively to assist school officers with providing safer routes to school for pupils; in other parts of London they are involved in facilitating the removal of graffiti, fly posting, fly tipping and acting as a professional witness in Antisocial Behaviour (ASB) cases. Some are also engaged in delivering presentations in schools to educate young people regarding the effects and costs of ASB.

### Police cadets

Police cadets in Haringey are another example of ways in which to support the police officers in school. A number of cadets received training in the British Sports Trust Junior Sports Leader Award. After successfully completing their course, six of them worked as mentors and role models alongside a group of young offenders at a nearby outdoor education centre. The week-long course focused on communication, teambuilding, and problem solving and challenged the participants to reflect on their attitudes and outlook on life. The cadets, several of whom had been in trouble with the police and received cautions themselves, were able to challenge the groups' behaviours and stereotypes and talk openly about the consequences of crime and issues such as peer pressure. (*Classrooms at War*, BBC Television Education, 24 May 2000)

### Sector officers

You will see that there are many different forms of support available to the schools officers, but probably the most important of these is that of the sector team officers who patrol the streets on a daily basis. Support from these officers is essential, as they are the first line of response should the schools officer require them. Since the inception of the schools officer post in its various guises over the past twenty years, school officers, in general, have seldom had to rely upon immediate police assistance. This has been due to the nature of their role in school, which has been mainly in the form of instructional lessons in the classroom. However, the new school beat officer role is fundamentally different and places the officer in a much more proactive and potentially dangerous role. It is therefore imperative that colleagues patrolling the street are aware of their existence and where and how they can best support them if the need arose. However, it appears from speaking to some schools officers that sector officers are unaware of their existence or role within the community and are often reluctant or sceptical about assisting them.

Several examples reinforce this concern: One officer who was working late at his school was informed that there were several suspects on the school roof, attempting to break into the school. He called for assistance to search for the suspects but was dismayed to find that officers took an unacceptable time to respond and then performed only a cursory search of the area, without tracing any suspects. The officer explained that he felt upset at the way in which the officers had conducted themselves and stated that they appeared disinterested, treating the call for assistance as an inconvenience. The officers left the scene and shortly afterwards the school officer, along with the school caretaker, discovered three pupils inside the school. Their attitude was the key indicator that made the officer feel isolated and undervalued at a time when he was performing a proactive role. It was as if the connection with schools or children devalued the importance of the call and the officers had arrived with the mindset that this would be an imposition and a waste of their time.

School officers have voiced numerous other examples, although there are a number of simple strategies which school officers need to apply to remedy this situation. As with any new role it is important that you announce it. Let other officers know what you are doing, whether it is by newsletters, intranet and or simply by speaking to them at training days or in the canteen. One school officer in Hammersmith and Fulham has used sector-training days to present a package to officers explaining his roles and responsibilities and where they can assist each other in the course of their work.

This can prove more difficult for some, especially when they take over a schools post at a new division. Some sceptics feel that, by avoiding this statement of intent, the officer is merely trying to avoid any extra work that may come his or her way now that the rest of the division are aware of their presence. Some school officers state that what concerns them more is the thought that if they call for assistance inside their schools they will be viewed as being unable to cope with a role that many view as merely chaperoning children. Others are concerned that school officials are extremely reluctant to invite any more police onto the school premises for fear of confrontation and public disorder.

What is of more concern is that, without support, the school officers cannot function effectively in their role; if we are not careful the school beat officer will continue to be viewed as a role which operates in isolation outside that of real policing. The police, as well as the public, need to be educated of the school officer's role. A good example of this was portrayed by one officer who made it his duty to answer calls when patrolling the local community around his school and to become actively involved in what was happening on the division. He would regularly come to the aid of other officers and invite other officers to come to his school. In return he was often invited to work with the local area car and was at the forefront of many of the arrests and incidents that arose on his patch.

## External links

### US police colleagues

It is useful to compare the relationship that the school resource officers in the US shared with their colleagues. It was quite unique and provided me with a real insight into how other people in the police department view their school-based colleagues.

As I described earlier the role of the SRO was traditionally one of educating children and being their friend. Consequently many people viewed their work as secondary to 'real' police work, where roles were distinctly more 'macho' and 'hands-on.'

I delivered a questionnaire to forty patrol officers in total at several 'roll calls', before embarking upon their day's tour of duty, in order to gain a better understanding of their relationship with the SROs.

### *Patrol officer questionnaire*

All of the officers were aware of the SRO partnership with the schools in the local area, although they admitted that it was to varying degrees. To confirm this, all but one of the officers was able to name their SRO as well as the majority of others in the department.

All but one was able to describe the role of the SRO and they all revealed that they had a very good understanding of what the SRO did on a daily basis. The patrol officers stated that the SROs worked full time in school and handled both civil and criminal issues, as well as being trained to deal with problems specifically involving children. Immediately they recognised the SROs as being specialists in their jobs and gave them recognition for dealing with caseloads that not only built up good relationships with the school, but that their work greatly assisted the patrol officers by reducing their workload. The patrol officers also identified them as a vital link between the police, school and the community and an important source of intelligence. It was also understood by these officers that the SROs, in addition to handling criminal matters, also spent a great deal of their time interacting with the pupils in an effort to prevent crime and to build up police/school relations.

The following quote from one officer sums up this understanding of the SRO role:

> 'A front-line officer that works with the staff and students at making a more positive impact at detecting crimes and making the schools a safe environment in which to learn. They are a great resource for patrol officers when working on juvenile crimes'.

It is this recognition that the SROs are front-line officers and not 'kiddie cops' that is so important and is a product of all the hard work which the SROs achieve on a daily basis.

> 'I think their statistics for calls handled, reports taken, and arrests made by SROs speak for themselves. They have their hands full.'

The SROs would regularly spend time with the patrol officers, both out on the street and also by attending roll calls, to exchange information with each other. This would provide the opportunity for the officers to highlight certain problems or 'hotspots' for crime in and around the school, and students who may be causing the trouble.

The SROs were always well received by the other officers and there did not appear to be any distinction between the two. There was often a relief expressed by the patrol officers that they did not have to deal with the juveniles and their parents as well as the school administration. In fact 81% of the other officers said that they would not want to be SROs; many of them cited their reasons as not enjoying working with teenagers.

> 'No, don't want to work with juveniles and don't want another group of supervisors, (i.e. staff from school)'

The patrol officers were all very complimentary about the way in which the SROs assisted them and, from the examples they gave of them working together on crime investigations, missing children, traffic reports and cases of child abuse, it was clear how well they worked as one unit.

## Volunteers

As well as linking up with ward and sector officers the school officer can also make full use of volunteers in policing. Many police forces, including the West Midlands, Thames Valley as well as the Metropolitan, now run volunteer programmes which provides individuals with opportunities to work with police officers and use their 'skills, experience, knowledge and enthusiasm to help the force reduce crime, disorder and the fear of crime in their communities'. (Thames Valley Police Volunteers, 2003).

The Home Office defines volunteers as someone 'who commits time and energy for the benefit of society, the community, environment and or individuals, undertaking freely and by choice, without concern or financial gain' (cited in West Midlands Police Volunteer Pamphlet, 2002)

These volunteers are a valuable asset for school officers who can use them to assist in their daily work in the school community. Many of the volunteers have skills which could help with delivering inputs to schools around personal safety, or crime and consequences. They could perform security patrols of the school or act as mentors to the school officers to encourage and support them and offer guidance and advice where appropriate. School officers could in fact be the first officers, with the exception of officers on the higher potential development scheme, to have their own personal mentors. Volunteers could also be used to take crime reports or host youth forums – or simply act as a liaison between the police and the school community.

In Fife, post office staff have been trained to report minor crimes and even collect fines over the counter; the Chief Constable is hoping to roll this out across the force.

There is great scope for the police service and, in particular, school beat officers to make full use of the skills and services that the volunteer community has to offer.

## Other external links

Fairbridge is an example of one such partner that the YOT work closely with and to whom school officers can refer young people. They are based in the most disadvantaged areas in the country, for 13 to 25-year olds who are not in education, training or employment, or who have been identified as being at risk of dropping out. The young people are referred to Fairbridge by numerous organisations (including the school police officers) and include those who have been excluded or involved in criminal activity. Each one receives a tailored programme of help.

'One in five of the young children who joined the Fairbridge programme was referred by a school, the education welfare service or community education'.

Fairbridge (2003)

## Youth Offending Teams (YOTs)

Much has already been said about the work of Youth Offending Teams and their links with school officers. A number of officers have forged good links with their respective YOT and it is now common practice for officers to notify them of young people with whom they may have concerns – in particular with regards to antisocial behaviour. In Haringey, officers have worked closely with Youth Inclusion and Support Panels (YISPs) to help disaffected pupils to take a more active role in school. On occasions YOTs have gone into school to work with the pupils alongside the officer and have attended the school's exclusion panel. In this capacity they have been able to draw on the services of other agencies, such as educational welfare officers and drug workers. The YOT has access to a number of such services and officers need to be aware of how they can link up with their local YOT and share good practice. This could include short attachments to the YOT during school holidays to get a better understanding of how they function and what they have on offer for young people.

## Connexions

This is a service available to all young people between the ages of 13 and 19 years of age, to assist them with a wide range of issues from school, friends and relationships to money, sports and music. Each young person is given a personal adviser who they can meet and discuss their concerns or issues with. Many schools now have their own Connexions adviser and school officers are working alongside a number of them to assist pupils with key areas that may be causing them concern. Many school officers have explained that Connexions workers are often based in the same room as them within the school, and that they have developed good working relationships with them when dealing with young people who are experiencing trouble with school life. Examples have included problems arising from truancy, bullying, drugs and street robbery as well as career advice. This is a good opportunity for school beat officers to use and share their knowledge and expertise with their partners and to develop the role of the Safer School Partnership.

For more information, visit their website at *www.connexions-direct.com*

## Fundraising

This is an area that always causes a great deal of anxiety for many officers as well as those whose intention it is to raise money, or seek funding, for projects and initiatives involving young people. On many occasions school officers explore the possibilities of producing educational packages or trips which engage young people; most recently, these have included resources for gun crime initiatives, to help address the growing number of incidents occurring in schools whereby children bring imitation or replica firearms into the playground. More often than not, school officers find that their work never leaves the drawing board because there appears to be no funding to develop their ideas.

What is more frustrating is that there are, in fact, numerous streams of funding available especially for schemes which acts as a diversionary tool in the fight against juvenile crime. The trick is to know how to successfully access such funding.  It is therefore proposed that there exists the opportunity for police officers in partnership with the school community to undergo some training in how to bid for such projects. A number of key issues are outlined in *Guide to Bidding* (Middleton J, 2004), where the steps to identify and win funding for a project or organisation are explained. It provides a guide to help those who want to access regeneration funding of various kinds: Lottery, European Social Fund or other local grants and funds. This ability to access money to fund such schemes is yet another important role for school beat officers, especially in terms of developing their own ideas – which are often unique to them, and not shared by others who do not have the expertise and understanding of their role.

## Role model

This fourth strand is one which has been referred to as an 'unofficial role'. (Atkinson, A 2000). It does however have a major role to play in the work of the schools officer and is something that has been developing over a number of years through contact with young people. This has been most notable as a result of work experience, police competitions such as drawing and painting on a safety theme and five-a-side football, and more recently with the expansion of the Volunteer Police Cadets.

Many schools officers, as well as police officers in general, forget the huge impact that their presence has upon young people – both in a positive and negative way. Initial meetings with officers can shape the way an individual behaves, interacts and views the police service and it is therefore critical that those officers – in particular schools officers – are aware of the opportunities that exist to influence these children and promote good citizenship amongst them. There are a number of ways in which this can occur. Among the most obvious are the ways in which officers talk to the children and treat them. Young people are very observant and critical of the way in which they are spoken to, and are very quick to accuse figures of authority who do not show them equal respect. They are also very aware of the way people dress and most young people are very respectful of a uniformed officer – although some view a uniformed officer as a visible threat. This is especially true of asylum seekers, refugees or immigrants who have their own perceptions of the police force from their experiences in their own countries.

Within this strand of 'role model' can be included the number of activities or diversions that schools officers can either be directly involved with or, alternatively, have a good working knowledge of, so that young people can be referred to them. This may be as a result of a child needing a club or activity to engage them after school rather than hanging around street corners and estates with nothing constructive to occupy their time; or simply to offer them opportunities to engage in to achieve something, obtain awards or make new friends.

This section seeks to explore some of these programmes on offer and provide the officer with an understanding and guide to a number of areas where they can divert, refer or encourage young people to explore and join in.

## The Prince's Trust

The Prince's Trust is a UK-wide charity, whose aim is to help young people to succeed. They target those young people, between the ages of 14-30, who are most in need of assistance.

According to their own literature,

> 'we help raise self-esteem, change attitudes, develop skills and support young people into work. In particular we target young people without jobs, with few or no qualifications, and those at risk.'

The Trust offers a number of programmes including:

- Volunteers Programme, a 12-week team-based course
- Business Programme, which helps fund and support young people to start their own business
- Group Awards, that give cash awards for young people working in the community
- Sound Live, a 6-day residential course that develops musical talent.

There are a number of others but two are of particular relevance to schools officers: the xl clubs and the Volunteers Programme.

**xl Club**

'A team-based programme of personal development for Year 10 and 11 students, based in schools'.

Prince's Trust, 2002

The xl club is aimed at tackling young people who are at risk of exclusion who may experience social or behavioural problems or who lack confidence or motivation. The programme is primarily for Years 10 and 11 and is run over a period of five terms. It provides pupils with the opportunity to take a fuller and more active role in school life by concentrating on areas that affect their lives, which they explore in depth. The programme is broken down into the following areas:

Personal, team and interpersonal skills

- Citizenship and community awareness
- Community project
- Entrepreneurship
- Residential
- Preparation for the world of work and work experience.

These programmes provide the adviser who organises the xl club with suitable training (two-day residential course), and support in the form of videos, handouts, newsletters, student portfolios, dedicated programme co-ordinator, contacts of other schools running xl clubs and a list of 'tried and tested ' activities.

One London schools officer in a secondary school ran an xl club for eight boys who had become completely disengaged with school life. Their punctuality and attendance was poor and on almost a daily basis they were taken out of lessons due to their disruptive behaviour. This resulted in them walking up and down corridors disturbing other classes and inevitably walking out of school and passing their time by engaging in antisocial behaviour on the local estates and parks.

The boys were taken every Friday by mini-bus to a local outdoor education centre where they focused on their behaviours and the effects that this was having on others with whom they came into contact. The classroom-based lessons looked at areas of communication, problem solving and team building and then attempted to apply the skills and knowledge gained in the classroom to outdoor activities.

These activities included communicating effectively with others whilst potholing in the dark and whilst negotiating a rock face. The pupils had to rely on teamwork and problem-solving skills to cross a river using lengths of rope and pieces of wood and similar skills to build a small floating craft.

Although the scheme was not officially evaluated, the pupils turned up on time every week and took a full and active part in both the classroom and outdoor activities. They enjoyed the scheme immensely and the officer noted that relationships between the pupils and the police was much more positive and productive. Several of the boys showed interest in the volunteer police cadets that was active in that borough and began turning up regularly to the evening sessions.

It is a worthwhile scheme for officers to undertake and with the training and support structure in place it offers a real opportunity to help challenge pupil behaviour and assist them in becoming active citizens within the school community.

The number of xl clubs in schools is constantly growing; over half of the schools that run them also have a full-time police officer stationed in their school. What is more surprising is that in many cases neither the schools officer nor the club organiser knew of each other's existence or the assistance or help that they could provide each other in terms of engaging these young people in school life.

The aim of the club is to improve motivation and attendance, which mirrors the aims of the Safer School Partnership; some officers have expressed concerns that this does not fall within their role as a schools officer – but it clearly does. The success and benefits of such a scheme can be highlighted by this case study.

*A group of girls from a West London school formed an xl club. The girls, according to their teacher, were clearly disaffected with school life and were regularly truanting and being very disruptive when they did attend school. The teacher who ran the club was a senior teacher who was very honest about the initial teething problems trying to encourage these girls to play an active part; at first, a number of them dropped out. Things soon began to settle and one of the first ideas that the club had was to do some voluntary work in the grounds of an old people's hospice adjacent to the school. The residents of the home had a number of concerns about the girls' school prior to their visit and it was made known that there were high levels of anxiety and fear of crime by the residents towards the girls, which was based on previous confrontations and the way the girls conducted themselves when out on the streets.*

*However, after several visits to the hospice the girls and the residents formed a number of good relationships; the girls invited them over to the school into some of their lessons. The result was that there was a significant reduction in the fear of crime amongst the residents and a mutual understanding and insight into each other's way of life.*

### The Volunteers Programme

'A 12-week team-based programme of personal development training'

This programme attempts to re-engage young people by helping them to focus upon what it is they wish to do with their lives and immediate future. The course comprises five key areas:

- Induction and residential team building
- Community projects and individual placements
- Activities to plan for the future
- Team challenge
- Final review and presentation.

Several police officers have run one of these programmes and although it has been very hard work it has also been extremely rewarding for them: they have developed and strengthened their own skills associated with organising a team of individuals, managed budgets and guided their teams successfully through a number of challenges. Schools officers are ideally placed to run such schemes with their knowledge, understanding and skills of communicating and motivating young people. However there is a significant time commitment and it may not be practical to devote such a large proportion of one's time to a single project. It is, however, a very beneficial project to the police officer *and* the recipients and one which is worthy of consideration. There is a police officer seconded to the Prince's Trust who can be contacted via the Prince's Trust website *www.princes-trust.org.uk*. There are also a number of officers who have run the programme and have developed briefing packages for officers considering the Volunteers programme.

## Volunteer police cadets

The volunteer police cadets are open to young people aged between 14-21 years of age. There are units in nearly all of the London boroughs and its members are drawn mainly from secondary schools and colleges, although some are referred by YOTs. The cadets usually meet once a week and learn about the role of the police service and participate in activities such as drill, physical education and the law. The aim of the units is to teach good citizenship and enable young people to develop their personal skills and qualities through structured training programmes. In addition to this, the units endeavour to enhance relationships between the police and local community and promote the police service as a viable career option for young people. The cadets are regularly deployed alongside regular officers helping out at non-confrontational events such as the Lord Mayor's show, the London Marathon or Trooping the Colour as well as undertaking local community parades and shows.

School officers have a role to play in the promotion of the volunteer cadets, as they are often the only link between young people and the police and are therefore in an ideal position to provide information on the existence and work of the cadet unit. In some local boroughs, cadet units have been attached to schools and acted as a feeder into the larger borough-based units. It is also worth noting that nearly half of all the volunteer cadet staff are in fact school officers who perform this role in addition to working in schools.

## Junior Sports Leader Award (JSLA)

This is another well-organised and structured programme that officers can assist with in schools, as part of the school programme or extended school activities. It was launched in 1994 by the Central Council of Physical Recreation (CCPR) who saw the need to provide young people with a formal sport qualification. The CCPR run a number of courses, but the JSLA, which is managed and developed on behalf of the CCPR by the British Sports Trust, is specifically aimed at young people over the age of 14. It forms part of the requirements for Key Stage 4 of the National Curriculum.

The British Sports Trust has five core values to its programme:

- Personal development: helping people reach their true potential
- A stepping stone to employment: providing them with a qualification to get started
- Developing leadership: teaching them organisation, motivation and teamwork skills
- Volunteering in the communities: encouraging them to help others
- Reducing youth crime: positive, safe activities keeping kids out of trouble.

For more information visit their website at: *www.bst.org.uk/*

### JSLA Project

**CASE STUDY**

In one north London borough a group of police cadets spent a half-term week being coached by a schools officer in the JSLA programme. The week was jointly supported by the local recreation department who developed a two-week summer programme for local children to come and play football, tag rugby, and kwik-cricket, which was run by the cadets. The aim of the scheme was to engage young people over the summer period and reduce the number of incidents of antisocial behaviour that take place in open spaces and parks – such as graffiti and criminal damage.

The cadets all successfully passed their JSLA course and the local children enjoyed two weeks of activities and received certificates at the conclusion of the programme. The council were keen to repeat the scheme and reported that there had been a decrease in the number of incidents of antisocial behaviour occurring in the parks.

## Duke of Edinburgh's Award

This well-known operation is a voluntary, non-competitive programme of practical, cultural and adventurous activities. It is designed to support the personal and social development of young people aged 14-25, and offers an individual challenge and encourages young people to undertake exciting, constructive, challenging and enjoyable activities in their free time.

The programme has five sections with three awards:

- Bronze (14 and over)
- Silver (15 and over)
- Gold (16 and over).

The sections include:

- Service: helping other people in the local community
- Skills: including a wide variety of skills, hobbies and interests
- Physical recreation: sports, dance and fitness
- Expeditions: training for, planning and completing a journey on foot, cycle, horseback or water
- Residential project (Gold Award only): a purposeful enterprise with people not previously known to the participant.

The programme is used extensively in many schools across the country and the benefits of such schemes for young people are widely recognised and include:

- Self-belief
- Self-confidence
- Sense of responsibility
- The ability to lead and work as part of a team.

For more information, contact: *Duke of Edinburgh Award Scheme* at *http://www.theaward.org/*

## Positive Activities for Young People (formerly SPLASH)

Splash is an acronym that originally stood for 'Schools and Police Liaison Activities for the Summer'. As it suggests, these schemes were led primarily by police officers but more recently the running of the programmes has been taken over by youth agencies including the YOT. The schemes are themselves administered by the Youth Justice Board and in 2002, high-crime estates in England and Wales catered for 55,000 young people participating in a range of activities. These included arts and crafts, football and drama workshops as well as outdoor activities: kayaking, rock climbing, sailing and DJ workshops. The list is extensive but the impact of engaging youngsters in such schemes appears to have had a significant influence on juvenile nuisance, which was reduced by 16%, motor crime was down by 11% and drug offences were down by 25%. More information is available in a Home Office publication *Summer Splash Schemes 2000: Findings from six case studies.* (Crime Reduction Series Paper 12)

The significance of these schemes for schools officers are founded on the relationships and knowledge that officers build up with young people throughout the course of their daily work. It is often police officers who are best placed to refer young people to such schemes and in their capacity as role models they can encourage and guide them into suitable activities and, where possible, assist and supervise in these programmes. There are, of course, concerns expressed by many officers that they do not possess the necessary sporting skills, and do not have either the cover or time available with flexible hours.

The government has now re-named the work of Splash as Positive Activities for Young People (PAYP), the new diversionary programme for young people who are deemed to be at risk of becoming involved with crime or at risk of social exclusion. The scheme will cost about £25 million in just its first year and will be supported by donations from Connexions, the lottery's New Opportunities Fund, the Youth Justice Board and the Home Office. This is good news for those families on low incomes who cannot afford to go out on trips or take holidays or finance visits to the swimming pool and cinema on a regular basis. One of the talking points raised by *Young People* magazine (White, P J 2003) is whether there should be more free activities for children during the long summer holidays to help low-income families. These families can often find summer holidays a real strain, as many single parents have to give up work to look after their children or, alternatively, pay for extra childcare and thus reduce their disposable income. The magazine also raises the issue of why the government targets children who are at risk of offending for these activities and not everyone else.

## Alternative schemes

There are also a number of other initiatives which are run by non-statutory bodies, and which police officers may be able to link in with. One of these is a scheme set up by two city businessmen, who decided to utilise the sports facilities at one of the country's most exclusive schools, St Paul's. It is known as the *Greenhouse Schools Project* and has programmes running in six London schools as well as Oxford and includes sport and drama-based programmes. It is all about giving access to good quality facilities and providing expert coaching for children from a number of areas; the children occupy their time and benefit in a number of ways from such an experience.

The work of Greenhouse also featured in *The Times* 'Sport' section (Syed, M 2003), which described the explosion of their table tennis club, which runs after school hours in Edgware School, north London. The club boasts over fifty pupils who compete against each other and according to the article, staff at the school are 'thrilled by the club's success and regard it as an essential factor in its quest to improve educational attainment'. This is a school where there are fifty languages spoken; a tenth of the school are refugees and 44% of all pupils require free school meals.

Schemes such as these are highly valued by the staff and it should not go unnoticed that they feel that they have a significant impact on 'educational attainment'. This, remember, is one of the key aims of the Safer School Partnership and it therefore follows that where officers can use their links with schools as well as their organisational and/or sporting skills to set up activities like this, then they will experience some of the many benefits that this article describes. 'Most of us play table tennis,' explains one boy. 'Without that opportunity it would be very easy for some to end up hanging around the estate, causing trouble.'

## Karrot

Karrot is a reward scheme devised by the Metropolitan Police in the London borough of Southwark, which aims to encourage young people to become active members of their school community and distance themselves from antisocial behaviour. The scheme has three main strands:

- A reward scheme that offers prizes to pupils for good attendance and behaviour

- A range of activities including football, cricket and 'DJ-ing'
- An Internet café, which allows children to access the Internet safely.

It is a partnership between the police and Southwark council, which focuses primarily on 11 to 15-year olds in the borough, and which both partners feel helps pupils play an active part in school life. School beat officers involved in the Karrot project have highlighted initial logistical problems with the scheme, especially during its implementation stages, but state that there are significant gains to be made in terms of developing relationships with pupils. the scheme has been heralded as one of several that has made a significant impact upon crime-related incidents amongst peer groups and level of absenteeism.

For more information, see the website at *www.karrot.org.uk*

## Police-led activities for young people

As already highlighted, there appears to be much debate around the credibility and effectiveness of officers involved in running activities for young people. However, it is apparent that many do so and are well equipped and suitably experienced and qualified – not only in their chosen activity, but also in their communication skills and ability to relate to young people who need it most. An example of this is an officer in Haringey who runs a boxing club for the local youth, many of whom are referred to him from the local Youth Offending Team.

One such individual who benefited from the club explains, 'I came to the police boxing gym for a week's trial and I have never looked back'. This young man is very open about his past in a YOI and his attitude to the police. 'It may look strange to an outsider to see a black kid taking lessons from a police officer – and in the old days I hated the police with a passion. But Gerry is different. He has a way of understanding everything and he is the first police officer that I feel comfortable around'.

Whatever one's feeling are on the subject of boxing, it appears that the existence of this club has made a genuine difference in this individual's life and has given him a real purpose and reason to get up in the morning, as well as helping him with his college education. He has been attending the gym for six months after having been involved with a number of street robberies; he has a contract with the officer to keep out of trouble. He knows that if he breaks this contract he will, among other things, be out of the club, which would probably be the most severe punishment of all. For him, his outlook has changed 'Life is about going to college, studying, getting something out of life and getting a job to work for the food you are eating'.

Obolie K, 2003 Evening Standard July 28th 2003 p103

Similar work has taken place in Sheffield where a joint initiative between Safer Schools, the YOT and professional boxing coaches has set up the Waltheof Boxing club. The scheme aims to address 'aggression management, drug abuse, attitudes to crime and the consequences of antisocial behaviour'. (Youth Justice Board, 2003)

The use of sport as a means of providing diversionary activity from crime and antisocial behaviour, and its ability to engage disaffected youth, has already been commented upon. Although many of the police-led activities are not evaluated, this should not detract from the good work that a number of police officers undertake.

Below are a few examples of schemes across the MPS that are either centrally co-ordinated or organised on a local basis and are due to the hard work and commitment of individual officers.

**Barnet**

In 1999, Barnet police ran a football coaching scheme in partnership with Power League and Barnet Educational Behavioural Management Team, as well as a highly successful five-a-side competition. They are also in the process of establishing a midnight basketball programme in partnership with the National Playing Fields Association.

**Brent**

Harrow are working closely with Watford FC, where they are providing coaching to local children as well as offering summer activities.

**Bromley**

Bromley currently have projects sponsored by the Thames Gateway, utilising Charlton Athletic FC for football events, and linking in with the local YOT to run midnight basketball. In addition, Volunteer Cadets, which includes YOT and school referrals as members, undertake various sporting activities on several weekends a year, including canoeing, swimming, rock climbing, and abseiling.

## Operation Athena Sport

Athena Sport was initially set up to focus on the issues around racism in sport, but soon expanded its horizons to encompass racism and diversity issues in all sport. Its work ties in with the MPS's 'safest city mission', vision and values ethos. Its mission is:

- To prevent and detect hate crime in sport within London
- To reduce fear of hate crime in sport in London
- To prevent and detect hate crime in London through sport.

The vision is:

- To make sport in London free from hate crime
- For sport in London to be a force against hate crime
- To harness sport in London in support of the MPS's 'safest city' vision.

In Brent they have formed the Brent Athena Sport Project, which is a police-led initiative set up by the local police Athena Sports liaison officer at the borough's partnership unit. Their aim is to promote anti-racism, racial equality and anti-homophobia in sport and to create an environment in which all people can participate in watching, playing, coaching and managing sport without facing discrimination of any kind.

To date they have run a social inclusion programme on a local estate using football as a sporting activity, and have initiated a sports database and an educational programme which they have piloted in a school in Brent, developing an educational and sports-based, activity-based programme.

There is a booklet entitled *Athena – Sport Spectrum Nov 2001: A menu for strategic and tactical options for combating hate crime in sport by the Metropolitan Police*, which outlines all the work of Athena Sport. Further information can be found by contacting Athena Sport or speaking to liaison officers who have been established in a number of London boroughs.

**Operation Athena Sport**
Room 934
New Scotland Yard
Broadway, London, SW1H 0BG
telephone: (020) 7230 4374
*Email: Op.Athena@met.police.uk*

## LIFE project at Shadwell fire station

In Tower Hamlets, London Fire Brigade are offering young people the chance to take part in a project called Local Intervention Fire Education (LIFE), which enables them to develop essential life skills. It is a one-week course, during which the attendees learn about commitment, teamwork, effective communication and punctuality as well as fire prevention and learning how to use fire equipment.

In addition, the course provides role models for the young people, as well as building relationships between the community and local fire service. Referrals are made to the course from Youth Offending Teams or the police or local school. The course has a passing out parade, when the achievements of the young people are demonstrated and certificates are awarded. Success has also been measured in a 46% reduction in the number of deliberately started fires across the borough.

London Fire Brigade are keen to expand the scheme and have highlighted the links that need to be forged between police, schools and themselves. The school community is in a unique position to help identify young people who may benefit from such schemes and the LFB have asked both police and schools to report instances where fires have occurred in schools or children have been seen playing with matches, so that they can help to educate the school and pupils about the dangers of fires.

Retrieved from Government Office for London website at:
*http://www.go-london.gov.uk/publications/annual_review_2003/shadwell_fire_station.asp*

## Fire Setter Intervention Scheme

This scheme is devised to address fire setting amongst children and young people aged up to and including 17 years. The scheme offers education and advice for young people and their parents, and visits are arranged to the child's home or a local community centre by trained advisers. It is important that school officers are aware of such schemes and are able to provide parents with advice about their children and their behaviour or fascination with fires. Officers should have an understanding of why children set fires, which includes natural curiosity and attention seeking, and the potential serious implications that may arise if such behaviour is not addressed. With 25% of all fires in London being started by children, officers need to be able to recognise the signs of regular fire setting:

- Small burn holes in carpets, charred paper in sinks or wastebaskets
- Matches or lighters hidden in cupboards and drawers or under beds
- An unusual fascination with fire
- Unknown fires in the school or home.

Retrieved from London Fire Brigade website at:
h*ttp://www.london-fire.gov.uk/fire_safety/schools_and_children/juv_firesetters.asp*

## Risk assessments

The need for risk assessments to be undertaken when engaging in any activities in particular of a sporting nature should be the first priority. No activities should commence without a full risk assessment being undertaken by a fully qualified risk assessment officer. In the MPS, all officers currently engaged in Volunteer Police Cadets have risk-trained risk assessment officers and examples of previous risk assessments for activities such as canoeing, rock climbing, football, swimming, excursions, camps and classroom sessions are posted on the intranet site to give officers an idea of the areas that they need to consider. There will be, in most circumstances, opportunities to conduct joint assessments with outside agencies – such as sailing clubs who will have their own risk assessment and health and safety policies. This should be a collaborative approach and cover all the potential hazards.

The Health and Safety Executive have published a guide entitled *Five steps to risk assessment*, which outlines what risk assessment is and the five steps to assessing it in your workplace.

- Step 1: Look for hazards
- Step 2: Decide who might be harmed and how
- Step 3: Evaluate the risk and decide whether the existing precautions are adequate or whether more should be done
- Step 4: Record your findings
- Step 5: Review your assessment and revise it if necessary.

For more information look at the website of the Health and Safety Executive at: *www.hse.gov.uk*

## The way forward

There are numerous other benefits which programmes such as those shown earlier can offer young people; it is in such work that schools officers may be able to assist. They are yet another essential tool in the diversionary programme and are already used by many of the Volunteer Police Cadet Units. It is here that officers can act as role models and, although the time devoted by an officer to schemes of this nature may be limited during term time, there does exist the opportunity to participate more fully in the holidays. There is concern, however, that police officers do not often become involved in sporting activities – for example, refereeing a football match after school or going on sports trips. This is due in part to the risk assessment that revolves around organising such events, but also the role that a police officer has to play, in terms of its effectiveness and appropriateness.

There are at present numerous schemes that take place across the country, which have been very successfully organised and run by police officers for a number of years. Many of theses schemes are sport-orientated and in many cases the officers run them in their own time – sometimes incurring a financial cost, but invariably with the intention of engaging youth and offering them a service which they would not otherwise receive.

While it is true that an essential part of the school officer's role is to promote diversionary activities in order to engage youth, there appears to be a consensus that officers may co-ordinate such schemes and oversee them in partnership with other agencies, but not be part of the coaching staff. This seems to fly in the face of much of the good work that is undertaken by officers, and appears contradictory to the work that officers are encouraged to participate with on the government's various summer programmes.

There needs to be some clear instruction around the extent to which officer should engage in such activities; whilst it is clear that it should not impose on their core duties as a school officer, there is clearly a need to utilise the skills of many officers who are highly qualified and extremely skilled and able to undertake such work. There also needs to be an appreciation of just how effective this work can be and there are a number of examples to highlight this.

# CHAPTER 6

# Further research

## University-based police officers

At present there are not enough officers to cover all the schools in the country with a minimum level of service, although the number of schools officers is clearly growing with the introduction of Safer School Partnership. What is now emerging is the need for a similar service to be adopted for universities and colleges across the country. Some may argue that this does not come under the remit of schools officers, although many university students are themselves still very young and naïve and, on an increasing basis, are finding themselves victims of assaults and burglaries. Who are better placed than schools officers, who have developed the necessary skills to work in partnership with educational facilities and have a good understanding of young people?

This is not a new concept; as early as 1986 Salford University adopted its own police constable who was responsible for the entire university campus, which included residential blocks, classrooms and a student/staff population of 12,000. He had his own office on site, which acted as a mini police station. (Wright, F 1986)

The officer concerned states that many of the students come from different walks of life and are simply not used to inner-city campus life. They stand out as students and are easy targets for pickpockets, burglars and sexual assaults. More recently, the National Union of Students mounted a campaign against the increasing number of racist incidents against minority students in higher education, especially since the exposed media coverage of terrorist incidents in the Middle East and in the wake of September 11. (Benady, A 2003)

A more recent example is that of Plymouth University, where Devon and

Cornwall constabulary has based its own full-time officer in order to provide students with advice on personal safety and crime reduction. (*Police Review*, 15 November 2002)

Greater Manchester Police have launched a game, which can be downloaded onto a computer by students attending Manchester University, which helps them navigate themselves safely from the university to the pub in an effort to promote their 'Street-Wise' project for students who are away from home for the first time. (Police Life, 2003)

There is now a section on the Home Office Crime Reduction website devoted to crime prevention around universities. The site is entitled *Good 2B Secure* and provides tips and advice about reducing the chances of becoming victims of crime at university. *www.good2bsecure.co.uk*

Research into this area has been conducted by Rosemary Barberet, Bonnie S Fisher, and Helen Taylor (2003) in a paper entitled *University Student Safety* and is available as publication F194.Uni.QXD on the Home Office RDS website at: http://www.homeoffice.gov.uk/rds/

## Teen courts

Teen courts are used extensively in the US as an educational tool for young people; it gives them the opportunity of participating in the judicial system. The programme is designed to allow students to understand more about the court system and to learn to respect and value it. Defendants are those who have already pleaded guilty and have been ordered by a court to attend a teen court for sentencing. They are normally first offenders, aged between 13 and 17 years of age, and referred to the programme by the relevant authority that deals with diversionary programmes. The court defers the sentence for each defendant that participates on the scheme and it is part of this deferment that they attend the teen court.

The defendant then has to appear before a court, which consists of teenage jurors and a defence and prosecutor 'attorney'. Adult coaches advise the attorneys, and direct them in points of law and ensure that the proceedings run smoothly. The teenage attorneys and jurors are all recruited from local schools and there is a requirement that all ex-offenders serve as jurors themselves and are actively encouraged to become student attorneys.

The trial determines the sentence for the defendant, which is decided upon by the teen jury; it will include components of community service and jury duty. In addition, the defendants may have to write letters of apology, essays or attend classes. In sentencing, the jury considers factors such as harm to the victim, the impact on the community, any aggravating factors as well as school performance and grades. They also consider the remorse shown by the defendant, previous conduct and school grades. The judge who presides over the sentencing oversees all of this.

The goals of the programme, taken here from the City of Lakewood Teen Court (2001) in Colorado, include:

- Exposure of juvenile offenders to a broader view of the criminal justice system
- Provision of a positive learning experience for youth, by offering them a chance to participate in the criminal justice system
- Provision of an excellent opportunity for legal professionals to act as mentors for the youth of the community
- Making juveniles accountable to their peers and community.

In the UK, potential recruits for the jury could be taken from the gifted and talented sections of children as well as mainstream and school beat officers could play an important function in helping to promote this scheme in partnership with the schools and local Youth Offender Teams as a good form of diversion.

## Exchange trips

There is still a great deal of scepticism by many schools officers about the effectiveness of school-based police. Much of this is founded on their own frustrations of embarking upon a new role – a role which is understood by very few and which is still in its infancy. Much of what these schools officers are experiencing was mirrored in the USA, who have over a number of years developed and refined their schools programme based upon what actually works. Much of their success has been as a result of building partnerships with the school community, which took a number of years to establish. The same will be true of programmes in the UK, but it may be of benefit for UK officers to experience, at first hand, some of the innovative programmes that currently exist in the USA. To enable this to happen, work is currently being undertaken to enable officers to visit the USA and work alongside American officers inside their schools. This will allow officers to exchange ideas and practices and give UK officers a real insight into how police/school programmes develop over time and become examples of good working partnerships in practice.

## National Association of School Beat Officers

This is a concept that already exists in other countries – most notably the USA, whose school officer association (aptly named National Association of School Resource Officers, website: *www.nasro.org*) boasts 7,000 members and holds annual conferences and training events throughout the year. It also provides a website that hosts a discussion page and has links to other useful sites. It is well-established and proves to be a valuable resource for the School Resource Officers, who are able to share ideas and viewpoints and provides a forum for these officers to promote best practice. This includes some disgruntled opinions expressed by officers, but it does help raise the profile of schools officers on a national level and gives them the support structure, which they need.

## Fixed penalty notices

New powers are now available to police officers to help combat yob culture in the form of fixed penalty notices. Although the use of such tickets is only being trialled in a number of pilot areas at present, the feedback appears to be very positive. Officers are able to give on-the-spot fines for nuisance and antisocial behaviour, which according to officers reduces paperwork and the amount of time spent dealing with such offences. The fines, ranging between £40 and £80, can be issued for offences such as dropping litter and it therefore raises the question of whether school officers will make use of these powers and issue tickets to children within the school community. (*Police Review*, 9 May 2003)

## Dispersal of groups and removal of persons under 16 to their place of residence

School officers need to be aware of legislation which may come into effect in the near future regarding young people. One of the more controversial aspects of the new Antisocial Behaviour Bill currently being considered is that of targeting young people who are hanging around streets and who are viewed by many local residents as being responsible for many of the problems around local estates. The Act will give police new powers to disperse groups of two or more and return young people under 16 who are unsupervised in public places after 9pm to their homes. There are conditions attached to this new power and relevant authority has to be sought to exercise it, but in effect police officers will be able to return young people to their homes if, between the hours of 9pm and 6am, they are found in a public place unsupervised by an adult. The degree to which this is used as a free taxi service remain to be seen, however...

## Training

It is clear that the role of school officers has changed dramatically in the past year, since the inception of the Safer School Partnership. Officers are now required to display a wide-ranging number of skills with which to undertake the role. It is one of the most demanding jobs for a police officer to embark upon and one which is still struggling to receive the recognition that it deserves from the police service.

To perform their roles effectively, school officers are receiving training in a number of key areas to assist them with their work; this is a major investment in a role that, if supported over a period of time by the relevant authorities and through a co-ordinated partnership approach, will undoubtedly result in reducing juvenile crime. School officers have a hard task ahead of them – but this is a programme that, although having many short-term goals, is set up to run over a lengthy period of time and reveal real long-term benefits for all.

# And finally...

With all of the skills outlined within this book, school officers – in partnership with other agencies – can make significant contributions to ensuring that schools become safer communities and that Safer School Partnerships thrive and be of benefit to all aspects of the community.

There are already over 200 school beat officers in the UK who undertake the majority of the roles described in this book. The success that such partnerships bring, in terms of making schools a safer community, are clear to see. For those of you reading this book who wish to mirror such work in your own area then Safer School Partnerships is the way forward. If you have any questions on how to set up such a partnership, are finding the development of one difficult, or need assistance on running any training, then contact me at *andy.briers@btinternet.com*

# Appendix

**METROPOLITAN POLICE** *Working for a safer London* | URN: PSP / / /

## PROBLEM SOLVING PROCESS – PSP

| Administration | | | |
|---|---|---|---|
| Department/Unit/Team | | | |
| | Name | Local Ref. (Pay no., etc.) | Telephone Number(s) |
| Person Leading | | | |
| Deputy | | | |
| Date Started | | Last Update | |

| 1 | The Demand |
|---|---|
| | 1.1 What is the demand? |
| | 1.2 Where is the demand coming from? |
| | 1.3 What is the significance of the demand? |

| 2 | The Problem |
|---|---|
| | 2.1 What is the problem? |
| | 2.2 Who are our partners? |

| 3 | The Aim |
|---|---|
| | 3.1 What is it you want to achieve? |

| 4 | Authorisation |
|---|---|

**Department/Unit/Team Manager**

Have checks been made to ensure that no one else is working on this problem?

Have appropriate background checks been completed?

I am the line manager and I ☒ ☒ support the need for action at this time.

My reasons are:

I recommend an assessment every:

Name:     Department:     Date:

Problem Solving Advisor's Comments (if one has been appointed):

| 5 | Researching the Problem |
|---|---|
| | 5.1 How is the problem currently being handled? |
| | 5.2 Who shares your problem? |
| | 5.3 Victim(s) |
| | 5.4 Offender(s) |
| | 5.5 Location(s) |

| 6 | Analysis | |
|---|---|---|
| | 6.1 | Victim(s) profile |
| | 6.2 | Offender(s) profile |
| | 6.3 | Location(s) profile |

| 7 | Problem Solving Meeting(s) |
|---|---|
| | |

| 8 | Options | |
|---|---|---|
| | 8.1 | Victim(s) |
| | 8.2 | Offender(s) |
| | 8.3 | Location(s) |

| 9 | Response | |
|---|---|---|
| | 9.1 | Victim(s) |
| | | Risk assessment for each intervention: |
| | 9.2 | Offender(s) |
| | | Risk assessment for each intervention: |
| | 9.3 | Location(s) |
| | | Risk assessment for each intervention: |

| 10 | Evaluation | |
|---|---|---|
| | 10.1 | Victim(s) |
| | 10.2 | Offender(s) |
| | 10.3 | Location(s) |

| 11 | Review | |
|---|---|---|
| | 11.1 | Has it met the aim? |
| | 11.2 | If yes, how has it met the aim? |
| | 11.3 | If no, why did it not meet the aim? |

| 12 | Closure | |
|---|---|---|
| | 12.1 | Comments/Observations by the Line Manager closing this file: |
| | 12.2 | Comments by Problem Solving Senior Manager (Lead): |

MP 983/03

# Glossary of terms

**ABC**            Acceptable Behaviour Contract

**ACPO**           Association of Chief Police Officers: develops policing policy at a corporate level. Membership includes Chief Constables, Deputy Chief Constables and Assistant Chief Constables or their equivalent in England, Wales and Northern Ireland.

**ASBO**           Antisocial Behaviour Order

**Audit Commission**   Appoints auditors to all local authorities and NHS bodies in England and Wales and helps bring improvements in economy, efficiency and effectiveness through value for money studies and audit process.

**BEST**           Behaviour & Education Support Team: multi-agency teams that work very closely with defined groups of schools to support teachers and provide early intervention, supportive services to pupils who have emotional and behavioural problems, and involve and support their families. Schools chosen for BESTs will include those with high proportions of pupils at risk of developing behavioural problems and of disaffection.

**CAMHS**          Child and Mental Health Services

**Connexions**     This service offers a range of guidance and support for 13 to 19 year olds, including a network of personal advisers.

**CPSV**           Center for the Prevention of School Violence, US-based

**Crime and Disorder Reduction Partnerships**   Established under the Crime and Disorder Act 1998 these are multi-agency partnerships tasked with producing local crime and disorder audits and strategies relating to crime and disorder issues. The police and local authorities are the lead agencies in these partnerships.

**Crime Concern**   A national not-for-profit charitable organisation managing a range of crime prevention and community safety projects and involved in training and consultancy for partnerships

**DARE**           Drug Abuse Resistance Education: a registered charity that promotes drug and violence education with a lifeskills-based programme

**DfES**           Department for Education and Skills: formed from parts of the former Department for Education and Employment (DfEE)

**DTO**    Detention and Training Order: one of the sentences that a court can give to a young person aged between 12 and 17 years. It is for a minimum of 4 months and a maximum of 24 months.

**FWS**    Final Warning Scheme

**Home Office**    The government department responsible for internal affairs in England and Wales through a system of inspections and the publication of thematic reports

**ISSP**    Intensive Supervision Surveillance Programme (ISSP): a programme supported by the YJB that aims to deal with the most active repeat offenders, and those who commit the most serious crimes. The programme's aims are to:

- tackle the underlying needs of offenders which give rise to offending, with a particular emphasis on education and training

- provide reassurance to communities through close surveillance backed up by rigorous enforcement.

**LEA**    Local Education Authority

**MPS**    Metropolitan Police Service

**NACRO**    National Association for the Care and Resettlement of Offenders: a crime reduction charity that seeks practical solutions to reducing crime, working with ex-offenders, disadvantaged people and deprived communities.

**NRU**    Neighbourhood Renewal Unit: set up in the Cabinet Office to co-ordinate the Government's Neighbourhood Renewal Strategy

**PRU**    Pupil Referral Unit

**PSHE**    Personal, Social and Health Education: part of the National Curriculum that incorporates a range of education areas including drug misuse

**SBO**    School Beat Officer

**SRB**    Single Regeneration Budget: a government funding stream

**SRO**    School Resource Officer

**SSP**    Safer School Partnership

**TES**    Times Educational Supplement

**YIP**         Youth Inclusion Programme: seeks to reduce offending, truancy, and exclusion in disadvantaged neighbourhoods. The projects do this by providing targeted assistance and support to the 13-16 year olds at most risk of offending, truancy or exclusion.

**YISP**        Youth Inclusion & Support Panel: local multi-agency planning groups involving representatives from Social Services, Education and Youth Service, Police, Health (CAMHS), Schools, Housing services, Connexions, Children's Fund services and YOTs, seeking to prevent offending and anti-social behaviour by offering voluntary support services for 8-13 yrs high-risk children and their families. The aim of the panels is to provide a multi-agency integrated approach to help at-risk young people and their families access mainstream services.

**YJB**         Youth Justice Board: monitors youth justice system, advises secretary of state, disseminates good practice, makes grants and commissions research.

**YOI**         Young Offenders Institution

**YOT**         Youth Offending Team: multi-agency groups set up under the Crime and Disorder Act 1998 to co-ordinate local responses to youth offending

# References

Atkinson Anne J (2000), *The Successful School Resource Officer Programme: Building Effective School and Law Enforcement Partnerships*, Greystone Publishers, Richmond Virginia

Audit Commission (1996), *Misspent Youth: Young People and Crime, Audit Commission*, London

Bamber D (25 June 2000), 'Widdecombe to campaign for police cadets at school' *The Sunday Telegraph*

Bamber D (30 June 2002), 'School sniffer dogs catch pupils on drugs' *The Sunday Telegraph*

Barberet R, Fisher B and Taylor H (2003), *University Student Safety, Home Office* RDS website **http://www.homeoffice.gov.uk/rds/**

BBC Television Education (24 May 2000), *Classrooms at War*

BBC News Talking Point (16 May 2001), *Police in Schools: Is it a Good Idea?* **http://news.bbc.co.uk/1hi/talking_point/1957381.stm.** date accessed 14/10/01

Benady A (12 Nov 2002), *The Guardian* – Education

Briers A N, (2003), International Journal of Police Science and Management, Volume 5 No 2

Briers A N (2003), *School-based police officers* (Unpublished PhD thesis, Middlesex University)

British Sports Trust (2001), Sports Leadership Award **www.thebritishsportstrust.org.uk**

Brown M (September 2002), *Teachers* Issue 22, DfES Publication

Center for the Prevention of School Violence (CPSV) (1997), Research Bulletin Volume 1, No 2, Raleigh USA

Center for the Prevention of School Violence, School Resource Officers (2001), *What We Know, What we think we know, What we need to know,* revised, Raleigh USA

Center for the Prevention of School Violence (2001), *Research Brief The Effectiveness of School Resource Officers* No 4, Raleigh USA

Center for the Prevention of School Violence (2001), SRO Web Forum, Raleigh USA

Challinger D, *Principals and police – a pilot study*, Australian Institute of Criminology

City of Lakewood (2001), *Teen Court in Colorado*

Clarke Brian (2000), 'New angle to tackle young tearaways' *The Times*

Community Orientated Policing Services training manual (2002), *National School Safety Center*, US Department of Justice

Connexions (2002), *My Connexions Handbook*

Crace John (13 March 2001), *The Guardian*

Crime Reduction News, July 2003

Crimestoppers Trust, 2003

*Daily Mail* (8 May 2001), Steve Doughty

Department for Education and Employment (1999), *Tackling Truancy Together: A Strategy Document*, DfEE, London

Department for Education and Skills Guidance (*Social Inclusion: Pupil Support*, Circular 10/99)

Department for Education and Employment (2001), *Together we can tackle it: A checklist for police and schools working together*, DfEE, London

Department for Education and Skills (2003), *'Promoting Children's Mental Health within Early Years and School Settings'* retrieved from **http://www.dfes.gov.uk/mentalhealth/section1.shtml**

Department for Education and Skills (2000 revised 2002), *Bullying – don't suffer in silence*

Department for Education and Skills (2002), *A legal toolkit for schools*

Doughty Steve (8 May 2001), *Daily Mail*

Duke of Edinburgh's Award (2002), Information pamphlet

*Enfield Independent* (20 August 2003), Southern K

*Evening Standard* (28 July 2003), p103, Obolie K

Fairbridge (2003), retrieved from **http://www.fairbridge.org.uk**

Farrington D (1996), *Understanding and Preventing Youth Crime*, Joseph Rowntree Foundation, York Publishing

Gottfredson DC (1998), *School Based Crime Prevention*, in Sherman LW, Gottfredson DC, et al *Preventing Crime: What works, What doesn't, What's Promising*, a report to the United States Congress prepared for the National Institute of Justice, College Park, MD: University of Maryland

Government Office for London Toolkit (2003)

Government Office for London (2003) **http://www.go-london.gov.uk/publications/annual_review_2003/shadwell_fire_station.asp**

Graham J and Bowling B (1996), *Young People and Crime*, Home Office Research Study No 145, HMSO, London

Gregory H, *Young People Now* Magazine (14 –20 May 2003), DfES Publication

*Guardian The* (13 March 2001), John Crace

*Guardian The* – Education (15 May 2001), Diane Taylor

*Guardian The* – Guardian Unlimited (15 July 2002), 'Law School' Weale S

*Guardian The* – Education (12 Nov 2002), Benady A

*Guardian The* (5 August 2003), White J

Home Office (1968) White Paper: *Children in Trouble*

Home Office (1987) Crime and Disorder Act

Home Office (1995) Arson Prevention Bureau

Home Office (1997) *School Security: Dealing with Troublemakers*

Home Office (1999) *Social Inclusion: pupil support*

Home Office (2001) *Police Stops and Searches: Lessons from a Programme of Research*

Home Office (2003) *A Guide to Antisocial Behaviour Orders and Acceptable Behaviour Contracts*

Home Office Crime reduction website, retrieved 2003 **www.good2bsecure.co.uk**

Home Office publication: *Summer Splash Schemes 2000: Findings from six case studies*, Crime Reduction Series Paper 12

Home Office Research Findings No 30 (1996), *Scare straight or educate*

Home Office Research Findings No 161 (1996), *Reducing Criminality Amongst Young People. A Sample of Relevant Programmes in the United Kingdom*

Home Office Research Study 201 (2000), *Tell Them So They Listen: Messages* from Young People in Custody

Hope for London Pamphlet (2003), produced by the Evangelical Alliance

The Howard League Penal Reform (2002), *Young People and Crime. A summary of The Howard League Consultation*

Hurst J (18 May 2001), 'Officer to clean up Damilola district' *Times Educational Supplement*

Lakewood Police Department August 2000 to May 2001, service locations for the school year

Lloyd C (1996), *Scare straight or educate*, Home Office Research Findings No 30, Home Office, London

London Fire Brigade, retrieved from **http://www.london-fire.gov.uk/fire_safety/schools_and_children/juv_firesetters.asp**

London Youth Crime Management Board (2002)

Metropolitan Police Service (November 2001), Athena –Sport Spectrum, a menu for strategic and tactical options for combating hate crime in sport

Metropolitan Police Service (2003), Drugs Strategy 2003-2006

Metropolitan Police Service (2003), Volunteer Police Cadets

Metropolitan Police (1998), *Guidelines for Police Officers Working With Education Establishments And Community Groups*, Metropolitan Police, London

Metropolitan Police Service (2001), *Police response to incidents in schools Draft 5,* Metropolitan Police, London

Middleton J (2004), *Guide to Bidding: Devising and structuring projects for grant funding*, Middlesex University Press

Mori Poll (2001), Research conducted for the Youth Justice Board

Mulraney S, *Home Office rejects full-time police presence*, Police Review (17 November 2001)

National Association for the Care and Resettlement of Offenders (1998), *Children Schools and Crime*, NACRO Publications, London

National Association Of School Resource Officers (1998), *Basic Course Manual*, NASRO, Florida

National Association Of School Resource Officers Survey (2001), NASRO, Florida

National School Safety Center (2000), Community Orientated Policing Services (COPS) *In Schools Keeping Our Kids Safe*, US Department of Justice Training Manual, Westlake Village, California

National School Safety Center (1995 Fall), News Journal *Education is everyone's business*, pp16-18

Obolie K (28 July 2003), *Evening Standard*

O'Connor L and Hayman A (2001), Adding value to school drug education? (A review of a national consultation and dissemination exercise following the ACPO/RIL Report) 1999, *Police Research and Management*, Vol 5, No 2, pp 33 – 44

Office of Juvenile Justice and Delinquency Prevention, Fact Sheet, March 2001

Owen G (20 May 2003), *The Times* p7

*Police Life* (November 2003), Vol 3, Issue 11

*Police Review* (February 1986), University Challenge

*Police Review* (15 November 2002), University Challenge

*Police Review* (9 May 2003), Untitled, p 10

Prince's Trust (2002), Information brochure

Research and Development Centre for the Advancement of Student Learning (Fall 2000), School Resource Officer Partnership Evaluation, Poudre School District

Routledge (1994), *School Bullying: Insight and Perspectives*

Safer School Partnership, Guidance, (2002)

Southern, K (20 August 2003), *Enfield Independent*

*Sunday Telegraph The* (25 June 2000), 'Widdecombe to campaign for police cadets at school' Bamber D

*Sunday Telegraph The* (30 June 2002), 'School sniffer dogs catch pupils on drugs' Bamber D

Surgeon General (2001), Youth Violence: A Report of the Surgeon General, Rockville, MD: Office of the Surgeon General

Syed M ((27 March 2003), *The Times* – Sport

Taylor Diane (15 May 2001), *The Guardian* – Education

Taylor M, *Study of the Juvenile Liaison Scheme in West Ham 1961- 1965,* Home Office Research Studies, (January 1971)

Thames Valley Police Volunteers, (2003)

*Times The* (2000), 'New angle to tackle young tearaways' Brian Clarke

*Times The* – Sport (27 March 2003), Syed M

*Times The* (20 May 2003), p7, Owen G

*Times Educational Supplement* (31 March 2000), Wendy Wallace

*Times Educational Supplement* (July 2000), Wendy Wallace

*Times Educational Supplement* (18 May 2001), 'Officer to clean up Damilola district' Hurst J

*Times Educational Supplement* (15 June 2001), Wendy Wallace

*Times Educational Supplement* (11 October 2002)

US Department of Justice (2002), *National School Safety Center*, Community Orientated Policing Services (COPS) training manual

US Department of Justice (2002), Office of Justice Programs Office for Victims of Crime, Reporting School Violence Legal Series Bulletin 2

Victim Support website, retrieved 19/02/03 http:/natiasso03.uuhost.uk.uu.net/latest.htm (August 2002)

Wallace Wendy (31 March 2000), *Times Educational Supplement*

Wallace Wendy (15 June 2001), *Times Educational Supplement*

Weale S (15 July 2002), 'Law School', *The Guardian* – Guardian Unlimited

West Midlands Police Advice Volunteer Pamphlet (2002)

White J (5 August 2003), *The Guardian*

Williamson D (May 2003), *Young People Now* Magazine

Wright F (1986) *Police Review*

Youth Justice Board (November 2001), *Risk and protective factors associated with youth crime and effective interventions to prevent it*, Research Note 5

Youth Justice Board (February 2003), *Youth Justice News*

Youth Justice Board (2003), *Crime Recording by Police Officers Working in Schools – Draft*

# Index